Memories of Mårbacka

SELMA LAGERLÖF

Memories of Mårbacka

translations from Doubleday, a division of Bantam, Doubleday, Dell Publishing Group, Inc.

compilation and notes by Greta Anderson

Penfield Press

Greta Anderson also selected works of Selma Lagerlöf included in *Invisible Links,* a Penfield Press publication of stories by Selma Lagerlöf. She graduated with honors from Stanford University, and received an M.A. and Ph.D. from Rutgers University. She studied poetry in the Iowa Writers' Workshop and works as an editor and landscaper in Iowa City, Iowa.

Associate Editors: Miriam Canter, Dorothy Crum, Dana Lumby, Diane Heusinkveld, Joan Liffring-Zug, Robin Ouren

Cover design by Robyn Loughran

Front cover photo of Mårbacka courtesy of Walter Pöppel and the Swedish Information Service. Back cover photo of Selma Lagerlöf and photograph of Mårbacka courtesy of the Swedish Information Service.

Line drawings throughout book by Johan Bull from *The Diary of Selma Lagerlöf.*

Other titles by Selma Lagerlöf available from Penfield Press:
POSTPAID *(Prices subject to change.)*

> *Memories of Mårbacka* $16.95
> *Invisible Links* $14.95
> *Girl from the Marsh Croft* $14.95
> *Three Stories: Scandinavian Kings and Queens*
>   *Astrid, Sigrid Storråde, The Silver Mine* $12.95

For a complete list of all titles, please send $2 to:
Penfield Press, 215 Brown Street, Iowa City, Iowa 52245

ISBN 1-57216-048-9
Library of Congress Number 95-72715

PREFACE

Selma Lagerlöf is best known in America and worldwide for her childrens' books, *The Wonderful Adventures of Nils* and *The Further Adventures of Nils* (1906–07). The success of these books, along with her other earlier works, enabled her to buy back Mårbacka, her beloved childhood home in the west-central province of Värmland, which the family's finances had forced them to sell in 1888. Three years after the *Nils* books, Lagerlöf won the Nobel Prize for Literature and was able to purchase the land surrounding the manor house. She dwelled at Mårbacka until her death in 1940.

The author's imaginative life was deeply rooted in this place and the people who inhabited it. The modest property had been in the family for hundreds of years and was imbued with a trove of stories and legends. Lagerlöf was thirty when Mårbacka was sold, teaching junior high girls in Landskrona while working on her first novel. About this experience, she wrote, "They say that a great sorrow or a deep loss is necessary to teach a person to write, and I experienced such a thing when my old, dear home had to be sold a few years ago. It has been since then that I taught myself to write, to throw myself, with my sorrow and joy, into my work." Likewise, the recollections of her youth that make up this volume, written when the author was in her sixties, seem to require the perspective of the "happy ending" of her return.

Lagerlöf's three volumes of memoirs follow a significant pattern. *Mårbacka*, the first volume, is devoted to family ancestral tales; in instances when she entered into the story, it is "Selma" or "the girl" she writes of. In *Memories of My Childhood*, Lagerlöf switches to first person in recalling the escapades of the children and grownups at the estate. The third memoir is in diary form. Clearly, Lagerlöf needed first to preserve her imaginative heritage, and only then to focus on her own thoughts and emotions. The order of stories in this book, however, introduces the reader first to the girl in her setting, then to the fairy-tale history of the place.

—*Greta Anderson*

CHRONOLOGY

1858	Selma Lagerlöf born, November 20, at Mårbacka.
1863	Grandmother, Lisa Maja Lagerlöf, dies.
1867	Visits Stockholm for treatment of lameness.
1873	Second visit to Stockholm, told in "The Stockholm Diary."
1882–1885	Studies at a teachers college for gifted women in Stockholm.
1885	Father dies.
1885	Works as a teacher at a junior high school for girls in southern Sweden at Landskrona.
1888	Mårbacka, the family home and estate, sold.
1891	First novel, *Gösta Berling's Saga*, published.
1894	*Invisible Links*, a collection of stories.
1895–1896	Travel in Italy and Europe—stipend from King Oscar II.
1897	Moves to Falun in the province of Dalecarlia.
1899	*Queens of Kungahälla,* about Scandinavian nobility.
1899–1900	Travel in Egypt and Israel.
1906–1907	*The Wonderful Adventures of Nils* and *The Further Adventures of Nils,* books originally commissioned by the government to teach schoolchildren Sweden's geography.
1907	Aunt Lovisa dies. Selma Lagerlöf purchases Mårbacka.
1908	*The Girl from the Marshcroft*, stories.
1909	Wins the Nobel Prize for Literature.
1910	Purchases the entire estate surrounding Mårbacka and becomes an active landowner. Lives there during the summers.
1914	Becomes a member of the Swedish Academy.
1919	Begins to live year-round at Mårbacka.
1922	*Mårbacka,* first part of her memoirs.
1930	*Memories of My Childhood.*
1932	*The Diary of Selma Lagerlöf.*
1934	*Harvest*, a selection of short prose.
1940	Dies, March 16.

Sources:

Edström, Vivi. *Selma Lagerlöf.* Trans. Barbara Lide. Boston: Twayne Publishers, 1984.

Larsen, Hanna Astrup. *Selma Lagerlöf.* Garden City: Doubleday, Doran and Co., 1936.

CONTENTS

It was a little homestead, with low buildings over-shadowed by giant trees. At one time it had been a parsonage, and it was as if this had set a certain stamp upon the place which it could not lose. They seemed to have a greater love for books and reading there than elsewhere, and a certain air of restfulness and peace always pervaded it. There rushing with duties and bickering with servants were never met with, nor was hatred or dissension given houseroom, either. One who happened to be a guest there was not allowed to take life too seriously, but had to feel that his first duty was to be lighthearted and believe that for one and all who lived on this estate, our Lord managed everything for the best.

— Selma Lägerlof, from "Story of a Story"

CHILDHOOD MEMORIES

...at Mårbacka there were no sorrows

In fact, there were: Selma, at the age of three, was struck with a lameness that never completely righted itself, and in time the precarious fate of the estate became clear. But the spirit of the place was gay and resilient, and it is this spirit, not the worries or failures, that shapes the author's memories. The physical handicap and the sense of impending loss only strengthen her determination to preserve her world in writing.

Mårbacka was a hive of activity where stories were always unfolding as well as being told. The children delight in this life; the young Selma's playmates include her older sister Anna and younger sister Gerda, and their cousin Emma Laurell. The governesses Aline Laurell and Elin Laurell also play important roles, while her two older brothers Johann and Daniel are further in the background.

This section opens with the accounts of Selma's becoming lame and a miraculous partial cure. Other stories, about the author's father, Lieutenant Lagerlöf, show him to be at the center of the young girl's imagination, just as his enterprises were often the hub of controversy on the estate. All of the stories reveal the resourcefulness of the Mårbacka inmates in devising amusements out of the modest fabric of their existence. The chief of these was storytelling.

— G. A.

THE NURSEMAID

Once they had a nursemaid at Mårbacka who was called Back-Kaisa. She must have been all of six feet high. She had a large-featured, swarthy, stern-looking face; her hands were hard and full of cracks, in which the children's hair would catch when she combed it, and she was heavy and mournful.

A person of that sort could hardly be said to have been especially created for the nursery, and indeed Fru Lagerlöf had deliberated a long while before engaging her. The girl had never been out to service and knew nothing of the ways of people; she had grown up on a poor backwoods croft, among the wooded hills above Mårbacka, far from any other habitation.

Probably there was no one else available, or Fru Lagerlöf would not have had her come. That the girl did not know how to make up a bed, or build a fire in a tile-stove, or prepare a bath, was understood beforehand, but she was teachable and did not mind sweeping out the nursery every day, or dusting, or washing baby clothes. What she could not seem to learn, however, was how to get along with the little folk. She never played with them or gave them a pleasant word. She knew no sagas, and no songs. It was not that she meant to be unkind, but she was so constituted that romp and frolic and laughter were hateful to her. She would have liked the children to sit quietly, each in his or her little chair, without moving or talking.

Fru Lagerlöf was at all events quite pleased with the nursemaid. As for her not knowing any stories—well, the Mårbacka children had their grandmother, who every morning as soon as she was dressed, gathered the youngsters about her and sang and narrated for them away up to dinnertime. And they had someone, too, who played with them, for Lieutenant Lagerlöf, whenever he had a spare moment, romped with his children.

Back-Kaisa was strong, patient, and dutiful. She was a
person to be depended on. When her master and mistress
went off to a party, they could rest assured that she did not
run out and leave the children alone in the nursery. If only
she'd had a more delicate touch she would have been
admirable. But hers were no gentle clutches when little arms
had to go into dress sleeves. When she washed the children,
the soap always got into their eyes, and when she wielded
the comb, they felt as if every wisp of hair were being torn
from their heads.

The nursery at Mårbacka was a light, warm, spacious
room—the best in the whole house. But, unhappily, it was a
gable room, and to get there one had first to go out into the
lower front hall, then up a flight of steps and across a big
attic. The attic stairs were steep, and difficult for little feet
to climb. The former nursemaid used to take a child on her
arm and carry it up, but Back-Kaisa didn't seem to know
enough for that. And it was positively terrifying to walk the
length of that attic—above all, after dark! So it seemed
almost necessary that little hands should have a large hand
to slip into. But Back-Kaisa, who had been accustomed to
the dark of the wild forest, probably thought the attic at
Mårbacka a nice safe place. She just stalked on and never so
much as put out a hand. One was glad if one could even catch
hold of a corner of her skirt.

The beds in which the three children slept had been made
by the clever old carpenter at Askersby. They were quite
decorative, with a little row of spindles across each head-
board, but they were in two sections that pulled out and
pushed in like a drawer. The three beds when open took up
a lot of space, so it was well they could be folded during the
day. That in itself was all right, but the clever old carpenter
managed to make the beds in such a way that they sometimes sprang apart in the dead of night.

When that happened, you were, of course, startled out
of your sweetest slumber. Finding your bed cut off in the
middle, you drew yourself into the upper end and tried to

12

catch back sleep again, but somehow it would not come. After a while, you stretched out your legs and let them dangle. In that position you lay waiting for the Sandman till you were as wide awake as in broad day. Then at last you decided to get up and try to push the two parts together. When you had apparently succeeded and had got the bed-clothes nicely straightened, you crept back into bed as cautiously as possible, and stretched out once more with a feeling of satisfaction. All went well, sleep came stealing on, then a careless turn and—crickety-crash!—the bed was apart again...which put an end to all hope of getting any sleep that night.

But Back-Kaisa slept peacefully through it all. It did not occur to any of the little ones that they might awaken her and ask for help. The former nursemaid had always jumped up the instant a bed broke down, and quickly fixed it without having to be asked.

Just over the nursery there was a little lumber-loft full of discarded looms and spinning wheels, and amid all that old rubbish lived an owl.

At night that owl made a dreadful racket. To the children's ears it sounded as if someone were rolling big, heavy logs over their heads. The former nursemaid used to laugh at them when they were frightened by the noise, and say there was nothing to be scared about—it was only the owl. But Back-Kaisa, who hailed from the forest, was afraid of all animals, furred and feathered. They were like evil spirits. So, whenever she was awakened in the night by the owl she would take out her prayer book and begin to read. Indeed she could not soothe the children, on the contrary, she terrified them so that the poor little owl grew into a huge monster with tiger claws and eagle wings. No words can picture how they lay shuddering to the very roots of their being at the thought of having a horrible ogre like that right above them. What if it should tear a hole through the ceiling with its great claws, and come swooping down...!

It can never be said of Back-Kaisa that she neglected the children, or beat them. But was that anything much? True, the former nursemaid had not been so particular about keeping them neat and clean, but she was oh, so good to them!

The children had three little wooden chairs which they regarded as their greatest treasure. These had been presented to them by the clever old carpenter of Askersby. Whether they were meant as compensation for his failure with the beds, they did not know, but they rather thought so. At any rate, the chairs were not failures. They were both light and strong, and could be used as tables and sleds. The children could ride them all around the room, stand upon them and jump to the floor, or lay them down and play they were a cow shed, a stable, or a rabbit hutch. Oh, there was nothing they could not be used for!

Why the children prized those chairs so highly could be seen at a glance by turning them upside down. On the bottom of each chair was the portrait of its owner. On one was Johan, a boy in blue with a long riding whip in his hand; on another posed Anna, a dainty little maid in a red frock and yellow leghorn hat—sniffing at a nosegay; while on the third was Selma, a tiny tot in a blue dress and striped apron, but with nothing in her hand and nothing on her head.

Now these portraits had been painted there to show to whom the chairs belonged, and the children regarded them as their property in quite a different sense from wearing apparel and other things they received from their parents. Their clothes traveled from one to another, and their nice toys were either locked away or set up on the corner bracket in the parlor, but the chairs, which bore their likenesses— who would have thought of depriving them of these?

Therefore, it was awfully mean of Back-Kaisa to put all three chairs on top of the high birchwood bureau, as she did sometimes, so that the children could not get at them. What if she had but just scrubbed the nursery and the little chairs would leave ugly marks on the wet floor if trailed across it? The former nursemaid never would have had the heart to take the chairs away from them.

Fru Lagerlöf saw, to be sure, that the maid did not understand her little ones and that they were afraid of her. But

Back-Kaisa had been hired for a year, and Fru Lagerlöf could not very well send her away before her time was up. She hoped, however, that things would be better in the summer, when the children could play out of doors and have less to do with the nursemaid.

One forenoon in the early summer, it happened that the youngest child, a little girl, had been left alone and asleep, in the nursery. On awaking she sat up in bed, half dazed, and wondered where everyone had gone; at the same time she felt singularly drowsy and uncomfortable. She remembered, as she came to herself somewhat, that earlier in the day she and the other children had been to Ås Springs with their father to bathe. On their return Back-Kaisa had put all three of them to bed—dressed as they were—that they might nap a while before dinner. But the beds on which Johan and Anna had lain now stood empty; so the little girl knew, of course, that they were already up and gone.

They were perhaps out in the garden playing? She felt a bit hurt at their running off like that, leaving her all by herself in the nursery. She had better crawl out of bed, she thought, and hurry down to them.

The little girl was then three and a half years old. She could easily open the door and walk down the stairs, but to cross the dangerous attic alone.... She listened. Perhaps someone was coming to fetch her. No, there were no footsteps on the stair; she would have to venture by herself.

But now that she wanted to rise from her bed she could not. She tried again and again, only to sink back. Her legs did not seem to belong to her; she had lost all control of them.

The child was terror-stricken. The feeling of utter help-lessness which came over her when the body refused to obey was something so dreadful she remembered it long, long afterwards—aye, all her life.

Naturally, she began to cry. She was in great trouble, and there was no grown person at hand to help or comfort her. But she had not been alone such a very long while when the door opened and Back-Kaisa appeared.

"Isn't Selma coming down to dinner? The big folk—" Back-Kaisa stopped short.

The little girl never thought about its being the cross nursemaid who stood in the doorway. In her desperate plight she only saw a grown person who could help her out, and put out her arms to her.

"Come and take me, Back-Kaisa!" she cried. "Come and take me!"

When the nursemaid came up to the bedside, the little girl threw her arms about her neck and clung to her as no child had ever done before. A little tremor went through Back-Kaisa, and her voice was not real steady when she asked:

"What's the matter with Selma? Is her sick?"

"I can't walk, Back-Kaisa," wailed the child.

Then a pair of strong arms lifted her up as easily as if she were just a tiny kitten, and all at once the stern, serious-minded woman knew how to talk to a little child.

"Naa—Selma mustn't cry for that! Back-Kaisa's going to carry Selma."

And with that it seemed as if all the little one's troubles had blown away. She was no longer afraid or unhappy. What did it matter that she herself could not walk when Back-Kaisa would carry her! And nobody had to tell her; she knew that one who had a good strong friend like Back-Kaisa was not so badly off after all.

THE BIRD OF PARADISE

They had taken, for the summer, a cozy little cottage at the end of Karlagatan, where they were so happy and content that Lieutenant Lagerlöf and the children named the place Little Mårbacka, which was the highest title of distinction they could bestow on a house in a strange city.

The little house fronted a bit of garden enclosed by a picket fence, and under the spreading trees, they had their breakfasts and suppers. At the back of the house were a couple of potato patches, beyond which, over against a high cliff, stood a tiny hut not much larger than the cabin on the *Uddeholm.*

In that hut lived their hostess, Fru Strömberg, who was the wife of a sea captain. During the winter months she occupied the cottage herself, but summers she always let it to visitors. She now sat in her tiny cabin from morn till night, surrounded by blossoming oleanders and tables and shelves laden with curios her husband had brought from foreign parts.

When Fru Lagerlöf and Mamselle Lovisa were having coffee with their friends and the Lieutenant had gone mackerel fishing, and when Anna had gone over to the candy man's daughters' and Johan to his crabs, Back-Kaisa and Selma would repair to Fru Strömberg's cabin.

Fru Strömberg was their special friend, and to sit with her under the oleanders was as restful as sitting with Grandmother on the corner sofa at Mårbacka. She could not tell stories, but she had many wonderful things to show them: big seashells that were full of sound and murmured when you put them to your ear; porcelain men from China with long pigtails and long mustaches; and she had besides, two very big shells—one a coconut, the other an ostrich egg.

Back-Kaisa and Fru Strömberg talked mostly of serious and religious things, which the child did not understand, but sometimes they touched on lighter subjects.

Fru Strömberg spoke of her husband and his voyages. He had a fine big ship called the *Jacob*, and just now he was on a voyage to St. Ypes, Portugal, to take on a cargo of salt. Back-Kaisa wondered how Fru Strömberg could have any peace of mind, knowing that her husband was drifting about on the perilous seas; Fru Strömberg replied that there was One who protected him, and therefore she felt that he was as safe on board his ship as when at home in the streets of Strömstad.

The kindly Fru Strömberg then turned to the little girl and said she hoped the captain would soon be at home, for there was something on the *Jacob* she thought Selma might like to see. They had a Bird of Paradise there.

"What is that?" asked the child, all interest now.

"It is a bird from Paradise," Fru Strömberg told her.

"Selma has heard her grandmother talk about Paradise," Back-Kaisa put in.

Yes, of course. She remembered that Granny had told her about Paradise, and that she (Selma) had pictured it as a place that looked like the little rose garden on the west side of the house at Mårbacka. At the same time, it was clear to her that Paradise had something to do with God. And now she somehow got the impression that the one who guarded Fru Strömberg's husband so that he was as safe at sea as on land was the Bird of Paradise.

She wanted so much to meet that bird. It might be able to help her. Everyone felt so sorry for her mamma and papa because she was not getting well. And to think that they had made this expensive trip only on her account.

She would have liked to ask Back-Kaisa and Fru Strömberg whether they thought the Bird of Paradise would do something for her, but she was too shy. They might laugh at her, she feared, but she did not forget what Fru Strömberg had told her. Every day she wished the *Jacob* would come, so that the Bird of Paradise could fly ashore.

Then one day she heard, to her great joy, that the *Jacob* had arrived. But she did not speak of this to anyone. To her there was something very sacred and mysterious about it all. Remembering how solemn her grandmother had been when telling about Adam and Eve, she did not want to tell Johan and Anna that on the *Jacob* there was a bird from Paradise which she was going to ask to cure her leg. No, she would not speak of it even to Back-Kaisa.

Now every time she went to see Fru Strömberg, she expected to find the bird sitting warbling in one of her oleanders. But he did not appear. "How strange!" she thought. One day she asked Back-Kaisa about it, and was told the bird was on the ship. "But you'll soon see it," said Back-Kaisa, "for tomorrow we're all going on board the *Jacob*.

It seems that Captain Strömberg had hardly been home a day before he and Lieutenant Lagerlöf were bosom friends. The Lieutenant had already been out on the *Jacob* several times, and liked it so well that nothing would do but the whole family must see what a fine ship she was.

When they set out, none of them had any real notion as to what boarding the *Jacob* meant. The little girl thought the ship would be lying alongside the quay like the big steamers. But indeed she lay in the offing. They had to get into a little boat and row out. It was strange to see that the nearer they got to the ship the larger she grew, till at last she loomed high as a mountain. To those in the rowboat, it looked quite impossible to clamber up *there*.

Mamselle Lovisa said straight out that if it was to that high boat they were rowing, she could not go aboard.

"Wait a bit, Lovisa," said the Lieutenant, "and you'll see it's easier than you imagine."

Then Mamselle Lovisa declared she would as soon think of climbing up the flagpole at Laholmen. She thought they had better turn back at once.

Fru Lagerlöf and Back-Kaisa agreed with her, and were for going home, but Lieutenant Lagerlöf stuck to his point. There was no fear but they'd get aboard all right, he said. This was perhaps their one chance to see how it looked on a merchant vessel; they ought not to miss such an opportunity.

"But once we're up we'll never be able to get down again,"

argued Mamselle Lovisa.

They met a boat laden with sacks.

"See that boat, Lovisa?" the Lieutenant said. "Do you know what's in those sacks?"

"My dear Gustaf," returned Mamselle Lovisa wearily, "how should I know?"

"Well, they're sacks of salt from the *Jacob*," the Lieutenant informed her. "They have neither arms nor legs, yet they've come off the ship, so surely you should be able to do it."

"You ought to dress up once in crinoline and long skirts," snapped Mamselle Lovisa, "then perhaps you'd not be so brave." They went on like that the whole way out to the ship.

The little girl who longed to meet the Bird of Paradise wished with all her heart that her father might induce her aunt and the others to go on board; though she, too, thought they could never in the world get up there.

All the same they presently lay-to under a swaying rope ladder. A couple of sailors jumped into the boat to help them with the climb. The first to be taken was the little sick girl. One of the sailors boosted her to his comrade, who bore her up the ladder and put her down on the deck; here he left her to go and help the others.

She found herself standing quite alone on a narrow strip of deck. Before her opened a great yawning hole, at the bottom of which something white was being put into sacks. She stood there a long while. Some of the folks down in the boat must have raised objections to climbing the ladder since no one appeared. When the little girl had got her bearings, she glanced about for the Bird of Paradise. She looked up at the rigging and tackle. She had pictured the Bird as being at least as large as a turkey, and easy for the eye to find.

Seeing no sign of it, she turned to the Captain's cabin boy, who had just come up, and asked him where the Bird of Paradise was.

"Come along," he said, "and you shall see him." He gave her a hand lest she might fall down a hole; then walking backwards, he led her down the companionway into the

Captain's cabin, a fine room, with polished mahogany walls and mahogany furniture.

In there, sure enough, was the Bird of Paradise!

The Bird was even more beautiful than her imagination had pictured it. It was not alive, yet it stood in the middle of the table—whole and perfect in all its gorgeous plumage.

The little girl climbed up to a chair and from there to the table. Then she sat down beside the bird and regarded its beauty. The cabin boy, who stood by, showed her its long, light, drooping feathers.

"Look!" he said. "You can see he's from Paradise, for he hasn't any feet."[1]

Now that seemed to fit in very well with her own concept of Paradise: a place where one did not have to walk but moved about on wings. She gazed at the Bird in adoration, her hands folded as in prayer. She wondered if the cabin boy knew it was the Bird that protected Captain Strömberg, but dared not ask him.

The child could have sat there all day, lost in wonder, but her reverie was suddenly interrupted by loud shouts from the deck. It sounded as if someone were calling, "Selma! Selma!"

Immediately afterwards, they all came rushing into the cabin—Lieutenant Lagerlöf, Fru Lagerlöf, Back-Kaisa, Captain Strömberg, Johan, and Anna. They were so many they quite filled the room.

"How did you get here?" they asked as with one breath — wonder and amazement depicted on their faces.

With that, the little girl remembered that she had walked on the deck, had walked down the stairs and into the cabin— that no one had carried her.

"Now come down off the table," said one, "and let us see whether you can walk."

She crawled from the table to the chair, and from the chair to the floor. Yes, she could both stand and walk.

How they rejoiced! Their hopes had not been in vain; the

[1]The first Birds of Paradise seen in Europe were mounted without feet (translator's note).

object of the journey was fulfilled. The little girl was not going to grow up a helpless cripple, but a normal human being.

The grown folk said it was the splendid baths at Strömstad that had wrought the change. With tears of joy and gratitude, they blessed the sea, the air, the city and all therein—glad they had come.

The little girl, meanwhile, had her own thoughts about it. She wondered if it was not the Bird of Paradise that had helped her. Was it not the little marvel with the quivering wings which had come from that land where feet were not needed that had taught her to walk here on this earth— where it was such a necessary thing?

THE "SLOM" SEASON

East of Mårbacka, beyond a wooded ridge, lies Gårdsjön, a little lake in which there is a fish we call *slom*. The fish is about two inches long, and so thin as to be almost transparent; but small as it is, it is edible.

In Lieutenant Lagerlöf's time, when everything was so much better than it is now, folks used to take this fish out of the lake in countless numbers. Its spawning time was in early spring, when the ice began to break and there was open water along the shores. One could stand at the water's edge and scoop the fish up with dippers and buckets. Certainly no one went to the bother of putting out nets for slom!

Slom was fished and peddled only at the spawning time; therefore it was a sure sign of spring when a Gårdsjö fisherman came to the kitchen at Mårbacka with the first catch. The man, knowing he had brought a desired commodity, boldly lifted the latch (in those days there was no lock on the kitchen door) and walked in with an air of confident assurance. He did not stop just inside the door as on other occasions; without stating his errand or even saying good-morning, he strode across the floor to the big table and deposited a small basket done up in a blue-checked cotton cloth. Then, stepping back to the door, he stood with head proudly erect and waited for what was to follow.

If the housekeeper and the maids were the only ones in the kitchen, he could stand a long while unnoticed, for they would not permit themselves to show any signs of curiosity. But if Lieutenant Lagerlöf's little daughters chanced to be there, they were over by the basket at a bound, eagerly untying the cover to see what was under it.

They found a little porcelain plate, edged round with a blue landscape, which they recognized as having seen every year at this season as far back as they remembered. On the plate was a small amount of slom—some forty or fifty fishes.

Now slom, when properly prepared, is a tasty fish, but for all that, it is considered rather common food. At the other manors in the district, it was looked upon as poor man's fare, but not so at Mårbacka. Lieutenant Lagerlöf was such a lover of fish he would hardly eat anything else the year round. After the eelpout had finished spawning in February, he had to be satisfied with such things as stock fish, dried pike, salt salmon, salt whitefish, to say nothing of the everlasting herring! So every day now he wondered if the slom would be along soon.

The little girls had also learned to regard this fish as a rare treat, and were delighted when they saw what was in the basket. They called to the housekeeper and the maids to come and see. It was slom! Lasse had brought slom! Wasn't it great? Wasn't it wonderful? And there was general rejoicing in the kitchen. The housekeeper immediately went into the pantry and made a sandwich for the fisherman. When handing it to him, she condescended to ask him whether it looked as if there would be a good "take" that year. The fisherman, cocky and self-satisfied (for this was his big day), actually had the temerity to chaff the dignified old housekeeper. He said there would be more slom than all the riches of Lieutenant Lagerlöf could buy.

Mamselle Lovisa, wondering what all this talk meant, came out to the kitchen. Instantly she caught sight of the fisherman and the plate of slom, she threw up her hands and exclaimed in despair:

"Good Lord! Is that awful stuff coming in now again!"

It was a great disappointment to the little girls that Aunt Lovisa did not share their delight. Still, she must have had some appreciation of the auspicious event, for she said something in a low tone to the housekeeper, who smiled and nodded approval. Whereupon the children and the maids were told not to let Lieutenant Lagerlöf know the slom had come; it was to be a surprise for his supper.

When the three little girls heard that, they were gladder than ever. Their father was their best friend and playfellow; there was nothing too good for him! They felt very important now, and not for anything would they leave the kitchen. They begged to be allowed to clean the fish, and knew from past years how it should be done: With one stroke you cut off the head, with another you drew out the "innards." The tiny fish had no scales or sharp bones. If you cut off the tail it was a sign you didn't know how slom should be treated. Even after the fishes were cleaned the children would not leave them out of their sight. They watched the housekeeper wash them, dip them in flour, and put them in the frying pan. It wouldn't do to throw slom in the pan just any way. The little fishes had to be laid down very carefully, one by one, close together, none overlapping, and fried hard, so that they all stuck together. Then, with a flip of the pancake-spade, they were turned over. When well browned on both sides, they were covered with a hard round oat-cake, and then turned out of the pan so that the slom lay on top of the bread. The housekeeper told the children that was the way their grandmother had fixed it. In the old mistress's time, they used to set before each person at table a round of slom on an oatcake, for in those days they were not so well-off for plates as now.

All the while the slom was frying, the children were on pins and needles lest their father should come into the kitchen. Every other minute, they ran out in the hall and opened the door to the living room a wee bit to see whether he sat quietly reading his newspaper. When he got up to go for his usual evening walk, their hearts were in their mouths. Oh dear! What if he should take a notion to go out by the kitchen way?

Later, at supper, the three little girls could hardly contain themselves. If they but glanced at their father, they began to titter. It was hardest for the littlest girl, who had to say grace. In the middle of the prayer, she gave a little chirrup like a sparrow when it sees a grain of corn. The Lieutenant was about to ask what had come over her when his eyes fell on the slom right by his plate. His face lit up.

"Thank the Lord we've got something to eat in the house once more!" he said, and actually meant it. For to him, only fish was food.

The children after their long silence broke into peals of laughter.

"Oh ho!" charged the Lieutenant, shaking a finger at them. "So this is why you've been running in and out the whole evening and wouldn't let me read my paper in peace!"

It was an unusually jolly supper. The Lieutenant was always good humored and talkative, but when he was especially pleased about anything, he became quite irresistible. Then he fairly bubbled with amusing anecdotes and kept the whole table convulsed with laughter.

As for the slom, there was no more than the Lieutenant himself could have eaten, but he insisted that all must have a share of this "delicacy." And, of course, everyone marveled that such a tiny fish could be so delicious.

"Now, doesn't it taste good, Lovisa?" he asked his sister, who was as fond of meat as he was of fish.

Even she had to concede, just for once, that like this it was not bad—but too much of it....

When the Lieutenant folded his serviette before rising from table, he said very solemnly:

"Now, Children, mind what I'm telling you: The King in his royal palace couldn't have had a better supper than we've had. So we must give God proper thanks for the food and not slur the grace."

Thus ended the first day of the slom season.

The next morning the Gårdsjö fisherman brought a whole pound of slom. He was well met, of course, and he asked twelve *skillings* the pound for his fish, which was considered a high price. The Lieutenant himself came out to the kitchen with the money in order to thank the old man for coming to Mårbacka with the slom, and request him to continue as he had begun.

"Now for pity's sake don't take it to the parson's or the founderer's!" he said.

This time, also, the little girls volunteered to clean the fish. And now they were repaid for the trouble. There was slom enough for the whole family at supper, and some for the

Lieutenant's breakfast. But the serving-folk did not have any that day, either; it was too choice a dish for them.

The third day, the fisherman delivered enough slom to fill a large earthen bowl. Slom was now served at the family table for both breakfast and supper, and in the kitchen it was set before the overseer, but not before the stableman or the farmboy.

The next few days, folk from every little hamlet along the lake came bringing slom to Mårbacka. The Lieutenant bought from all. Soon every earthen vessel in the cupboard was filled to overflowing, and the fish had to be emptied into a huge copper kettle; when even that would not hold it all, it was dumped into a big vat.

But to clean such a lot of small fish was no light task! The housemaids had to leave off spinning and weaving to sit in the kitchen cleaning slom. The three little girls were no longer to be seen in the schoolroom. It was not for fun they cleaned slom now, but to help the grownups. Fru Lagerlöf and Mamselle Lovisa put aside their other work to give a hand. But it was a bit of a change for them all—a little departure from the usual routine.

The housekeeper did not help clean fish, she stood at the stove the whole day frying it. Before long she began to complain of the quantities of butter the fish was taking. The butter tub had been full only a few days before, and she could already see the bottom. That was the first break in the general satisfaction.

The family had slom for breakfast and slom for supper, but thus far at dinner there was the usual Värmland midday fare—corned beef or pork, or herring balls, or fried ham, or sausage, or whatever else there was on hand. But such fare was not to the taste of Lieutenant Lagerlöf. One day when he was served meat that had lain in brine since autumn, he lost all patience.

"I don't see why we should sit here and eat salt food when the pantry is full of nice fresh fish," he flung out. "But that's always the way of these fine housekeepers; they feed the homefolk on salt stuff and let the fresh things stand on the

27

shelves and spoil, waiting for company."

That was a sharp rap at his sister. But Mamselle Lovisa took it calmly; she was too fond of her brother to be offended by anything he might say. She meekly answered that she had never heard of anyone's setting slom before guests.

"I know, Lovisa, that you are too refined to eat slom. You have been out in the great world, and know how things ought to be. But I don't see why we back here at Mårbacka need bother ourselves about what they do in Karlstad or Åmål."

A light broke in on Mamselle Lovisa. "But surely you don't want slom for dinner, too!" she exclaimed, as if such a thing were unprecedented.

"Certainly I'll eat slom whenever I can get it. Why do you suppose I buy it every day, if I'm not to have any myself?"

After that, they had slom morning, noon, and night, which was not a happy thought on the part of the Lieutenant. There is no denying that slom is a nice-tasting fish, but it has an unpleasant odor. Not in the sense of being tainted, but it is evil-smelling from the moment it comes out of the water. However, all that disappears in the frying. But those who have to handle the raw fish cannot escape, for it is an odor that clings. Do what you will, it stays by you. Everything you touch smells of slom.

Soon all but the Lieutenant began to sicken of slom. They took smaller portions at each meal, and sighed as they sat down at table and saw the everlasting slom set before them again.

Lieutenant Lagerlöf, however, went on buying. The fisherman who had brought the first mess, true to his word, came faithfully every day, and sometimes twice a day, but his manner was noticeably changed. He now pulled the latchstring very gently, and came in with a meek and deprecating smile. He did not set the fish on the kitchen table, but left it outside the door. Though he removed his cap and said goodday, he had to stand and wait for a good half hour before anyone seemed aware of his presence.

Pleasant as it had been for both the maids and the children to escape for a while from the old routine, they were by now so sick and tired of cleaning fish they longed to get back to their regular tasks. None of them would so much as look at the fisherman.

"I say, Lars, you're not bringing slom again today, are you?" the housekeeper once asked him, as if he were offering stolen goods.

The man just blinked his eyes; he was too abashed to utter a word.

"We've got more fish now than we can eat," she told him. "I don't believe the Lieutenant wants to buy any more of that horrid stuff." However, she knew the Lieutenant was not to be trifled with in the matter of slom, so she had tell him the fisherman had come.

One day the Lieutenant was out when the old man appeared, so the housekeeper peremptorily ordered him away. All in the kitchen were glad, thinking that for once they would not have to clean any slom. But as luck would have it, the old man met the Lieutenant in the lane, and the latter bought his whole bagful of fish and sent him back to the house with it.

It went on like that for a couple of weeks. Everyone was weary and disgusted—except the Lieutenant. He chanted the praises of slom at every meal; it was wholesome and nutritious food. One need only look at the fishermen down in Bohuslän who lived on fish; they were the strongest and healthiest men in the whole country.

One evening Mamselle Lovisa tried to tempt him with larded pancakes, a favorite dish of his. And no wonder, for such larded pancakes as the old housekeeper made you never tasted in all your life!

"The overseer and the men, I suppose, must have their fill of slom, so you want me to be satisfied with pancakes!" The Lieutenant waved away the plate of nice hot cakes.

"Oh, no, that's not the reason," said Mamselle Lovisa. "The overseer and the men are so sick of slom we dare not set it before them."

Then the Lieutenant had to laugh, but, as he would not touch the pancakes, they had to fetch him some slom.

29

Toward the end of the second week, the whole household was in open rebellion. The housekeeper raged about the inroads on the butter, and the servants declared they could not go on working at a place where they fed you nothing but slom. It had reached a pass where the Lieutenant dared not show his face in the kitchen, for there the murmurs were loudest. Nor were things as they should be in the dining room. Joy had fled the board. The governess left her plate untouched, and the little daughters of the house—who otherwise stuck by their father through thick and thin—even they, began to pipe a few feeble protests.

Then at last Fru Lagerlöf came to the rescue. She conferred with Mamselle Lovisa and the housekeeper, and they all thought it time now to resort to the old tried and sure remedy.

At dinner there was boiled slom. Now, the very look of boiled slom is enough! There is a pallor about it peculiarly corpselike, and, besides, it is quite tasteless. Just the sight of it takes away one's appetite.

When the Lieutenant saw the boiled slom he looked as glum as the others.

"We are all out of butter," Mamselle Lovisa gave an excuse, "and since you will have slom at every meal we had no choice but to serve it boiled. For may part," she added, "I think it tastes no worse that way than any other."

The Lieutenant made no answer; so they all knew that Mamselle Lovisa had triumphed. He might easily have stepped into the pantry and seen for himself whether the butter was all gone, or ordered a fresh supply, but he did neither.

After that dinner, he bought no more slom. What was the use, he said, when the womenfolk were too lazy to prepare the fish in the proper way? No one contradicted him, though all knew he was as glad as they were to see the last of the slom.

THE VOW

Oh, why doesn't Papa come home? He went away the day after we had been to the prayer meeting at the inn and has not been at home since. We miss him dreadfully. There is no one now who talks to us at dinner; no one who plays with us in the evening after supper. Nurse Maja says he is out collecting taxes and has only been gone a few weeks, but to us it seems as though he has been away for months.

Then, one morning, Mamma tells us that Papa is coming home today, and we are overjoyed. Many times that day, we run out on the porch to watch for him and to listen for his sleigh bells.

"Don't keep running in and out, children," Mamma says, "or you'll catch cold." But we don't care.

Aline Laurell scolds us because our minds are not on our lessons. "If I did not know who was coming this afternoon, you would all get bad marks."

Gerda is busy dressing her dolls the whole livelong day. She dresses and undresses them again; she can't seem to make them fine enough to suit her. Anna and I assure Emma Laurell that Papa has toys for her as well as for us. She doesn't know our papa if she has any doubts about that.

At four o'clock, when lessons for the day are over, Aline tells us we need not read our lessons for tomorrow. She knows, of course, that we couldn't learn them anyhow. Anna, Gerda, and I, and Emma Laurell, too, all rush out to meet Papa. But first we run down to the stable to get the big ram that Johan drove for us last Christmas, and harness him to the sled. The snow is nearly gone, but we know that Papa likes to see us drive the stable ram.

What luck! We have hardly reached the avenue when we hear the jingle of sleigh bells. Now he is coming! We recognize the horse, and the wide sledge, and Magnus the driver, and Papa, himself, in his big wolfskin coat. We barely have time to push and pull the ram out of the way, for he is not sufficiently broken into harness to turn aside when he meets a horse. He plants himself in the middle of the road, rises on his hind legs, and thrusts his head forward, ready to drive the horse into the ditch.

How strange that Papa does not stop to greet us! I thought he would take Gerda and me into the sleigh, or at least let Gerda ride to the house with him, but Papa only nods his head ever so little and drives by.

We are sorry now that we took the ram out, as we are in a hurry to get to the house, and the ram doesn't know enough to turn round when we pull on the rein. All four of us have to stand on one side of him and push till he understands what he must do. That is why we were too late to receive Papa when he pulled up at the curb. But why he did not wait there for us, we can't understand.

We storm into the hall—no, he isn't here. He must be hiding somewhere. We are about to rush into his room, when the door opens and Mamma comes out.

"Go quietly upstairs, like good children, and stay in the nursery. Papa is ill and must go to bed. He has a high fever." Mamma's voice trembles so, as she speaks, that we are frightened.

After we have crept upstairs and gone into the nursery, Anna says that she thinks Papa is dying.

In the evening, when we're all in bed, Mamma always comes up to hear our prayers. We say an "Our Father," and "Lord Bless Us and Keep Us," and "God Who Cares for Little Children," and "An Angel Watches over Us." She goes from bed to bed and we each repeat, in turn, the same prayers— first Anna, then Emma Laurell, then I. Emma Laurell also prays God to bless and keep her mamma and her brothers and sisters and all good people. But tonight Anna also ends her prayer like Emma: "Dear Lord, bless and keep my papa and mamma and my brothers and sisters and all good people."

Anna says that because she wants God to protect her papa, who is sick. Mamma understands and bends down and kisses her. Then Mamma goes over to Emma Laurell, and after Emma has said an "Our Father," and "Lord Bless Us and Keep Us," and "God Who Cares for Little Children," and "An Angel Watches over Us," she prays as usual for her mamma, her brothers and sisters, and for all good people, but at the very last she says: "Dear God, spare good Uncle Lagerlöf, and don't let him die as You did my papa."

When Emma Laurell has said her prayers, Mamma bends down and kisses her also. Then she comes over to my bed, and I say an "Our Father," and "Lord Bless Us and Keep Us," and "God Who Cares for Little Children," and "An Angel Watches over Us," but I can't say any more. I want to, but words fail me. Mamma waits a moment, and then she says:

"Aren't you going to pray God not to take your papa from you?"

I want to—oh! I want so much to say it, but I can't.

Mamma waits a little longer. I know she is thinking of all Papa has done for me. It was for my sake he went that time to Strömstad; for my sake too, that he sent me to Stockholm for a whole winter's treatment at the Institute. And yet I can't get a word across my lips. Mamma rises and goes away without kissing me.

But after she has gone, I lie thinking that perhaps Papa will die because I did not pray for him. Perhaps God is angry because I did not ask Him to protect my papa, and will take him away! What can I do to show God that I do not want my papa to die?

I have a little gold heart and a small onyx cross which Mamselle Spaak gave me. If I give these mementos away, perhaps God will understand that I do so that my papa may live. But I'm afraid Mamma might object to my parting with these keepsakes. I shall have to think of something else.

The doctor has just been here. Soon after he left, Mamma told us that Papa had inflammation of the lungs. She said that one night while Papa was away from home, he had to sleep between damp sheets, which was the most dangerous thing one could do.

Aline Laurell helped Mamma to nurse Papa last night, and today, too, she has spent most of the time in the sickroom. Mamma doesn't know what she would do without Aline, for she is clearheaded and calm. Aunt Lovisa, on the contrary, is so dreadfully afraid Papa will die that Mamma can't have her in the sickroom.

After assigning our lessons for the day and giving us long sums in arithmetic to do, Aline went down to Papa's room, but she did not come back to see whether our answers were correct. At last we children, finding it too dreary to be alone in the nursery and so far removed from all the grownups, steal downstairs to Aunt Lovisa's room.

Auntie sits at her sewing table reading in a big, thick book, with Gerda on a low stool at her side making a dress for her doll. We three, Anna, Emma Laurell, and I, crawl up on Auntie's sofa and sit there quietly. We think it strange that Gerda can play with her dolls on a day like this. But then Gerda is too young to understand that her papa is dying.

We feel easier since we came into the kitchen bedroom. Everyone thinks Aunt Lovisa's room so cozy. They all say it is a bit of the old Mårbacka. Here is the wide bed where Grandfather and Grandmother had slept, and there, in the corner, is the tall grandfather clock, and near it stands the pretty bureau the clever carpenter at Askersby made for them from the wood of an old apple tree and the old syringa grown at Mårbacka. The cover on Auntie's sofa Grandmother made with her own hands, and the intricate pattern she learned from Aunt Wennervik, who was married to Grandmother's brother. The chair on which Auntie is sitting was Grandfather's own desk chair, and the mirror on the dresser, with a veil hung over it, was also made at Askersby. The tall wooden urns, filled with dried rose leaves, on either side of the mirror, Auntie bought at the auction at Valsäter, where her sister Anna—she who was married to Uncle Wachenfeldt—had lived.

There is nothing in the kitchen bedroom that Aunt Lovisa

would part with except, perhaps, the ugly black trap door over the cellar stairs. But when Papa talks of taking it away, Auntie says he'd better let it stay since it is so old. She would not feel at home in her room if the trapdoor were missing.

On the wall above Auntie Lovisa's bed hangs a picture of a white church in a grove of towering trees, and a low cemetery wall with an iron gate enclosing a churchyard. That picture, however, is not painted but clipped. It was Aunt Anna Wachenfeldt who wielded the shears. Aunt Lovisa says that picture is so skillfully cut out and pasted together that it is really a work of art! But I think it looks tawdry. Around the mirror there are four small canvases which Auntie herself painted when she was in boarding school at Åmål. One represents a rose, the second a narcissus, the third a carnation, and the fourth a dahlia. These, I think, are very pretty. Aunt Lovisa still has her box of colors and her pencils, but she never paints any more pictures as pretty as these. Auntie also has another picture which hangs above the sofa. It represents a stout boy and a stout girl out rowing in a small round boat into which they can barely squeeze. The whole picture is worked in cross-stitch on canvas. Aline Laurell says that Aunt Lovisa ought to take it out of the frame and make it into a cover for a sofa cushion, but Auntie will not change anything that is old; so it must hang where it hangs.

Over by the window stand three tall oleander trees full of bright red blossoms, and on the wall hangs a little book rack which is just large enough to hold the prayer book, the New Testament, *The Love Life*, by Johan Michael Lindblad, and the thick book that Aunt Lovisa studied when she went to school at Åmål. All she needed to know of French, geography, Swedish history, nature study, and domestic economy was contained between the covers of this book.

We see Aunt Lovisa dash away a tear, but she goes on with her reading just the same. Sometimes Gerda rises from her stool and asks Auntie whether she should put black or white trimmings on her dolly's dress.

"Dear child, do as you like!" But after a little, Auntie is sorry she spoke hastily, and tells Gerda what she wants to know.

I am wondering, all the while, what I should do so that God will let my papa live. I should like to ask Aunt Lovisa's advice about this, but I am too shy.

Before long, the housekeeper comes in with a tray.

"Have a wee drop of coffee, Mamselle Lovisa," she says. "You need it when there's so much sadness here. Not that the Lieutenant is dying..."

"No, Maja, I can't drink any coffee today." Then, thinking it would be ungracious of her not to accept when the housekeeper had gone to the trouble of preparing the coffee, she lays the book aside and pours out a cup for herself.

As she does so, I rush over to see what that thick book she is reading might be. All the other books in the house I am familiar with, but this one I have never seen before. It is a large, bulky volume with a stout binding of brown leather, warped and faded, and a brass clasp and mounting of brass. But the title is in such curious lettering I can scarcely decipher it.

"Oh, see!" the housekeeper exclaims, "the Paymaster of the Regiment's Bible! It's many a year since I've seen that Book, and I have wondered what had become of it."

"That Bible has been in the cupboard of my attic storeroom since the death of my mother," says Aunt Lovisa, "but today I decided to take it out."

"You did right, Mamselle Lovisa. The Paymaster always declared that that Book was better than all the doctors and all the medicines in the world."

"Aye, that Book was his solace in every need. Do you remember, Maja, that Father used to say he had read this Book cover to cover at least fifty times?"

"Yes, indeed, I remember it well," the housekeeper answers. "And I remember, also, how peacefully we went to sleep of a night when we knew that the Paymaster of the Regiment lay reading his Bible in here! It seemed as if no harm could come to us."

When Auntie and the housekeeper said that Grandfather had read the whole Bible fifty times, I looked up. "Does Maja think God was pleased with Grandfather for reading the Bible through so many times?"

"You may be certain that He was, Selma."

On receiving this assurance, something extraordinary comes over me. It is not anything that I, myself, have thought of, but rather as if someone had whispered into my ear what God would have me do in order that Papa may recover.

I hesitate at first—the Book is so dreadfully thick. What if it contains only sermons and admonitions? Well, what matter, if it saves my papa's life? Folding my hands, I make a solemn vow to God that if He spares my father's life, I will read the Bible from cover to cover, and not skip a single word.

I have no sooner made my vow than Mamma comes to the door. She looks more hopeful now than she looked last night.

"How good of you, Lovisa, to take charge of the children!" Mamma, apparently, is not aware that we have run away from our lessons. "I came to tell you that Gustaf has taken a sudden turn for the better. His fever has abated, and he is no longer delirious. It may be some time, however, before he is out of danger, but with God's help I think he will be spared to us."

I don't think it was so hard for Grandfather to read the Bible through fifty times as for me to read it only once. Grandfather could sit down to read whenever he wished. Grandmother furnished lights for him to read by, so that he could lie down and read his Bible evenings.

If I were to tell Mamma or Auntie that I had promised God to read the Bible through so that Papa would get well, perhaps I, too, could have a light to read by at night. But it wouldn't do for me to speak of this to anyone. Once there was a princess who had twelve brothers who were changed into wild swans, and in order that they might become human again, she had to knit them each a shirt of stinging nettle yarn. The nettles pricked her fingers and tore her hands, but she dared not tell why she was doing it, nor do I.

The doctors at the Institute in Stockholm ordered me to rest for an hour every day after dinner. This is what Papa always made me do when I was little. So, during the rest hour, I read the Bible. Not for long, however, as Mamma always comes to tell me I must close the Book and go to sleep awhile.

Anyhow, I'm glad that Aunt Lovisa does not carry the Bible up to her attic storeroom and lock it away in her wardrobe. I think it was God who ordered it left on the shelf of the yellow corner cupboard above the trapdoor to the cellar. That cupboard is never locked, and I can take the Book as often as I wish.

Aunt Lovisa says it is well that I am reading the Bible, for under the lid of her sewing basket, she reads when no one is looking. Once or twice, I borrowed one of these novels and forgot to return it, but now that I am reading the Bible, her novels are not disturbed. Mamma and Aline Laurell do not approve of my reading indiscriminately. Once they took away from me a book entitled *The Woman in White,* just as I had come to the most exciting part. But Mamma and Aline have no objection to my reading the Bible, for the Bible is the Word of God.

It is a good thing, too, that spring is here with its white nights. On Sundays we don't have to rise before eight, and I can lie and read the Bible for several hours. But the Book is so long it seems as though I could never finish it.

Gerda sleeps in the bedroom below-stairs, but she always comes up to the nursery before she is half dressed, and wants to play at toss and catch with pillows. She can't understand why I lie here reading and do not want to play. It makes her very sad. I am sorry, but it can't be helped. One has to endure harder things than this if one is to read the whole Bible at ten years of age.

I wonder at times if Grandfather read every word in the Bible, as I am doing. I read the genealogy and all the laws, and everything about the sacrificial rites, and about the Tabernacle, and the vestments of the High Priest. I also wonder if Grandfather could pronounce all the strange words, and if he understood everything he read.

I have read in the biblical history most of the things recorded in the Bible. I know all about Adam and Eve, the Flood, the Tower of Babel, and also about Abraham and Joseph and David, but I am reading it again, word for word, since that is what I promised God.

It is Sunday morning. Anna, Emma Laurell, Gerda, and I are out walking. It is the only thing we can do during the month of May. The winters are much jollier, for then we can go skating or sledding or drive the stable ram. Even April is better than May, for one can dig canals in the wet snow on the country road, or dam up waterfalls in the brook. But in May there is nothing to do but gather wood anemones, which may be fun for a day or two, but we have already tired of that. Now we just walk along the road, having as dull a time of it as if we were grown folk.

Anna and Emma Laurell are walking on one side of the road, talking in low tones. Their talk is of boys and of pretty dresses. Such things they seem to think Gerda and I are too young to understand. We walk on the opposite side of the road, and I'm telling Gerda about a beautiful play I once saw at the Royal Dramatic Theatre in Stockholm, called *My Rose of the Forest*.

All of a sudden, Anna and Emma come over to our side. They, too, want to hear about the play. "It must have been wonderful," they exclaim. Emma Laurell then tells us that in Karlstad, when her father lived, she and her sisters used to dress up and do theatricals. And Anna says that perhaps we, too, might do them here some day.

"Why not today?" says Emma Laurell. "Uncle Lagerlöf is well enough to be up, and we have gone over our lessons for tomorrow."

We face about quickly and almost run home to play *My Rose of the Forest* talking and planning all the way. Before we reach the avenue, most of the parts have been assigned.

39

Emma Laurell is to play the young girl who is called My Rose of the Forest, because she has pretty red cheeks. Anna is to play the young gentleman who is in love with her. She is pale and has dark hair, which is suitable for a lover. The Old Man of the Forest, with whom Emma Laurell lives, I'm going to play, for I have long white hair, just like the Old Man at the theatre. But where shall we find someone who can play the Old Man's housekeeper? Gerda won't do, as she is too small for the part. Finally we decide to make up with Nurse Maja—although she kept us waiting at the inn while she stood on the barn steps gabbling with Lars Nylund—and let her be the housekeeper.

Gerda is disappointed because she is to have no part to play, and begins to cry. We feel uneasy, for once Gerda starts crying she'll keep it up all day. The grownups might think we had been mean to her, and forbid us to play theatre. Therefore, we tell Gerda that she may play a little brother to Emma Laurell and sit on a stool and dress her dolly. She is content with that, thank goodness!

When we come home, we have to listen first to the reading of a sermon! But just as soon as it is over, we tell Mamma that we are going to play theatre, and Mamma lets us have the key to the big closet in the garret. We hunt up all sorts of discarded clothing, which we try on. It's heaps of fun.

The nursery is our stage, and the scene is supposed to be a big forest in which there is a small cottage enclosed by a high wall. We can't have the forest or a cottage, but we must have the wall for Anna to jump over when she comes to court Emma Laurell.

So we build a wall of all the beds, bureaus, tables, and chairs in the nursery and cover it with blankets and quilts to make it look like a wall. For without that wall, it would be impossible to do the play as it was done in Stockholm. It is awfully hard to make the wall stand; it keeps tumbling all the while. The actors, when not on the stage, will have to stand by to hold the wall up.

The audience is to sit out in the garret. No curtain is necessary, as we have only to open the door of the nursery for the spectators to have the whole stage before them. Inside the wall, we have placed a table, a chair, and a stool on which Gerda is to sit. We hope everyone will understand that the table, the chair, and the stool represent the cottage where My Rose of the Forest lives with her grandfather. We rehearse the play once. I tell Anna and Emma Laurell the lines they are to speak. Emma Laurell can hardly keep from laughing, and I fear she will ruin the play, but Anna is excellent.

As we are about to begin the performance, Uncle Kalle Wallroth and Aunt Augusta arrive from Gårdsjö to see whether Papa is well enough to go with them to Filipstad to Aunt Julia's wedding. How provoking! Now neither Mamma, nor Aunt Lovisa, nor Aline Laurell can come to see our play! They will have to entertain Auntie and Uncle. But when Auntie and Uncle hear that a play is to be presented that has been given at the Royal Dramatic Theatre in Stockholm, they want to see it, too. Then Papa suddenly becomes interested. He puts on his fur coat and escorts them up to the theatre.

It is too bad we must have Gerda on the stage dressing her dolls when she doesn't belong in the play! As soon as we open the door, ready to begin the performance, Papa asks Gerda what part she is to play, and Gerda answers as if she were herself and not the small brother of My Rose of the Forest. And Nurse Maja is no good, either, for she overdoes her part. She has borrowed the housekeeper's big Paisley shawl and carries a cane, with which she thumps the floor as she walks, and she is all bent over, and grins horribly, so that she looks like an old hag.

But Emma Laurell is charming; so is Anna. Anna is wearing a military jacket that Papa had worn in the days when he was a cadet in Stockholm. Her hair is drawn up under a military cap, and we have painted a black mustache on her. Emma is wearing Mamma's white satin wedding dress and has her hair hanging.

I have long, hanging locks, too, like the Old Man at the Dramatic Theatre, and am wearing a short jacket which

41

Johan has outgrown, and the long bloomers I wore at the Institute. So I think the audience will know that I am the grandfather.

I'm so glad that Anna got over the wall without knocking it down or stumbling, for the whole play hinges on that.

Once, when I'm on the stage scolding Emma Laurell for allowing Anna to scale the wall, I hear laughter out in front and, looking round, I see Gerda shaking her forefinger at a doll—mimicking me. Never again will she be included in any of our theatricals!

Emma Laurell acts well, but she has a big smudge on her upper lip where Anna kissed her. The rest of us can scarcely keep from laughing. When the play is over we receive more applause than the actors who played the piece at the Dramatic Theatre.

Afterward, we have to put everything in order, both in the nursery and in Mamma's attic closet; so it is some time before we are through. When at last we come downstairs, Mamma says that Papa is tired and has gone to bed, but he would like to have us come to his room. And we go at once.

"Thank you, children," he says as we stand by his bedside. "I want to tell you that this has done me more good than all Dr. Piscator's pills."

And that, of course, is the best news we could have. Then we go into the parlor to pay our respects to Uncle Kalle and Aunt Augusta. They, too, are pleased with our performance and say they have had such a good time.

We begin to think we are wonderful. Uncle Kalle pats me on the head and chucks me under the chin. "So this is the girl who directed the play," he says in his usual jovial voice. I expect him to praise me and say it was awfully clever of me to coach the others in a play produced at the Royal Dramatic Theatre in Stockholm. But instead, he says in sepulchral tones, "But are you not supposed to be a little pietist who carries a big Bible around with her everywhere?"

I feel too embarrassed for words, but I can't tell him why I'm reading the Bible. Uncle, seeing how disappointed I am, pats me on the cheek as he adds, "Auntie and I haven't laughed so heartily in many a day. The next time you come to Gårdsjö you must give that play there."

I understand that Uncle Kalle wants to comfort me, but just the same I'm dreadfully uneasy. What if Papa should hear that people are calling me a pietist?

There is so much to be endured if one reads the whole Bible when one is only ten years old!

Aline Laurell has borrowed a novel from Fru Unger of West Ämtervik which is said to be very entertaining. She has lent it to Mamma and Aunt Lovisa, and they are so eager to see how the story ends they can hardly lay the book down. I have seen the book both in Mamma's room and in Aunt Lovisa's. It is entitled *A Capricious Woman*, and is by Emilie Flygare-Carlén. How I should love to read it!

One Sunday morning the book lay on the dining room table for several hours, and I could have read many chapters, but I did not open it. Until I have read the Bible through, I will not begin another book.

It is a good thing, too, that summer is here. Aline and Emma Laurell have gone home to Karlstad. As we have no lessons now, I can read the Bible for several hours every day. But the summer is also troublesome, for Daniel and Johan are at home from school. And, of course, they have been told that I'm reading the Bible, and are forever teasing me about it.

"Listen, Selma," they say, "you who read the Bible, do you know where Jacob went when he was in his fourteenth year?" Or, "Do you know, Selma, what the twelve apostles are doing in the Kingdom of Heaven?" Or, "Can you tell us who was the father of Zebedees's children?"

But what does it matter? You have to put up with more than that if you read the whole Bible when you're only ten.

Papa is up and dressed, but he lies on the sofa two or three hours every day. He feels tired and weak, and his cough still hangs on. He says he may never be himself again.

Papa, Mamma, and Anna have been to Filipstad to Aunt

Julia's wedding, but the journey didn't do Papa any good, and now Mamma thinks he should go to Strömstad for the summer, and take the baths for the sake of his health. But I know that it is not necessary. He will get well anyhow as soon as I've finished the Bible, but I can't tell this to anyone.

Perhaps God has made it possible for Papa to go away so that I may continue the reading. So long as Papa is not himself, we don't tell him anything that might upset him. Therefore no one at home has told him that people think I was converted by Paulus of Sandarne when I heard him preach at the inn, and that I am now a pietist. But maybe he'll hear of it anyhow. What shall I say if Papa asks me why I am reading the Bible? It won't do to lie about it, and it won't do to tell him the truth.

It is well, at all events, that the summer nights are long and light. As soon as Mamma has heard our prayers and Anna has gone to sleep, I crawl out of bed and sit by the window to read for hours and hours.

Papa has come back from Strömstad, hale and strong as he was before he went tax collecting and slept between wet sheets. We are all so glad he is home again!

We have many guests in the house just now—oh, so many! Uncle Schenson and Cousin Ernst and Klaës and Alma are here, and Uncle Hammargren and Aunt Nana with Teodor, Otto, and Hugo. Then, too, we have Uncle Oriel Afzelius and Aunt Georgina with their children, Elin and Allan, besides our bachelor uncle, Kristofer Wallroth.

Aline and Emma Laurell have also come, not to start school, however, but to be here on the seventeenth of August, when Papa will be fifty years old.

It is glorious weather, and the fruit this year is abundant. The gooseberries and currants are ripe; so are the cherries, and the greenings are almost ready to pick.

What a pity I have not finished the Bible yet! I'm reading the Book of Revelation now, so I'm almost at the end. But with so many guests in the house, there's not a corner where

I can sit down to read for an hour in comfort and peace while I finish the Book.

But, fortunately, Mamma has suggested that they all go up to Storsnipan this afternoon to see the beautiful view. When both children and grownups have gone, and I am alone in the house, I run into the kitchen bedroom and take the Bible out of the corner cupboard. Then, hurrying out to the garden, I seat myself under a gooseberry bush where I can eat gooseberries while reading the Book of Revelation. I'm so glad the Book is nearly finished and I won't have to keep any more secret vows.

In the midst of my reading, I hear footsteps approaching, and, glancing up, whom should I see but Uncle Kristofer! And I thought he had gone with the others to Storsnipan! When he sees me sitting under a gooseberry bush with Grandfather's big Bible in my lap, he comes straight over to me. I tremble with fear when he asks me what I am reading, but I tell him, of course, that I am reading the Bible. And then he wants to know how much of the Book I have read, and I tell him that I have read it all but the last few chapters of the Book of Revelation, which I am reading now. He makes no comment, but from the look on his face I know that he is ready to burst out laughing.

When he has gone, I close the Bible and carry it back to the kitchen bedroom and replace it on the shelf of the corner cupboard. I know well enough that when Papa and Uncle Schenson and Uncle Hammargren and Uncle Oriel return from Storsnipan, Uncle Kristofer is going to tell them that he found me seated under a gooseberry bush reading the Book of Revelation. And when Uncle Kristofer relates anything, he makes it so screamingly funny that the listeners laugh themselves sick.

I rush into the kitchen to help Aunt Lovisa and the housekeeper prepare supper. I run out to the kitchen garden and gather parsley and dill, and into the pantry for onions and pepper. In fact, I run all possible errands so as not to be seen when they come, or to hear Uncle Kristofer tell them how amused he was to find me sitting under a gooseberry

45

bush reading the Book of Revelation.

There is much to do when the house is full of guests, and after supper, I help with the dishes so that I may stay in the kitchen until my bedtime.

When we have many guests we children do not sleep in the nursery. Aunt Nana, Aunt Georgina, and Aline Laurell occupy it now. Anna, Emma Laurell, and Alma Schenson have to content themselves with a big closet in the garret, while I sleep on the sofa in Mama's and Papa's room.

Sometime in the night, I am awakened by hearing my name—Mamma and Papa are talking about me.

"Did you hear what Kristofer said about Selma?" Papa asks—not as if he were angry, but only amazed.

"Yes," says Mamma, "and I think he might have let the child alone."

"I've been away all summer, but you must have noticed whether she reads the Bible habitually."

"She has been reading the Book the whole summer, both early and late."

"But, my dear Louise, don't you think you should have forbidden her? Anyhow, that is no reading for a child."

"No, of course not," Mamma replies, "but Aline and I thought it best to leave her in peace."

"Then I shall have to talk to her myself," says Papa. "I don't want her to become an evangelist."

"No, Gustaf, you mustn't."

"But I don't understand...."

"Well, you see, I think she is reading the whole Bible in the hope that you may be restored to health."

"Oh, it isn't possible," says Papa.

"But you know how unhappy she was when you were stricken. She took it harder than any of the others, and ever since she has been diligently reading the Bible."

"Oh, it isn't possible," Papa says again. He clears his throat several times, as if it were hard for him to get the words across his lips. "It isn't possible that the girl is so simple-minded."

Mamma makes no answer, and Papa says nothing further. I know that I may read the Bible as much as I like, since Mamma stands up for me. But I never take down the Book from the shelf to finish the few pages in Revelation which I have not read.

Now that the mystery has been revealed, there is no power in the thing I vowed. It would be useless, therefore, to go on with the reading. So, what was the good of it all?

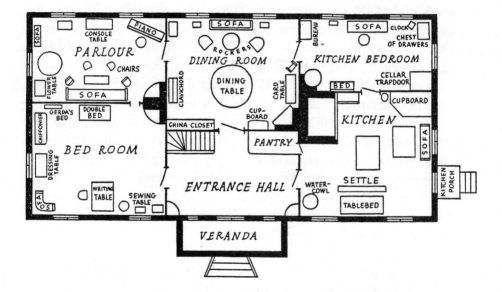

Ground-floor plan of the manor house at Mårbacka

THE EASTER WITCH

In the middle of the afternoon of Easter Eve, two maids always steal out of the kitchen, each with a bundle of clothing under her arm, and go down to the cow barn. They do it as secretly as possible, so that we children won't notice anything unusual. But we know, all the same, that they are going to make up an Easter witch, because Nurse Maja has told us all about it.

Down there in the cow barn they hunt up a long narrow sack and stuff it with straw. That done, they dress the sack in a soiled and ragged old skirt and jacket, the poorest they can find—one that is threadbare and out at the elbows into the bargain. The sleeves of the jacket they also fill with straw, to make the arms look natural and plump. For the hands, they pull some straw below the sleeves.

After that the maids make a head for the Easter witch of a coarse gray kitchen towel, tied together at the four corners, and fill it, too, with straw. They sketch the eyes, nose, mouth, and two or three wisps of hair with charcoal, and then top the head with an old screen bonnet which the housekeeper puts on in summer when she is going to capture a swarm of bees.

When the witch is ready, the maids carry her up to the house. They dare not bring her inside, however, but stop at the foot of the steps leading to the porch. They fetch a kitchen chair in which they set her down, and then run over to the brew house for the long oven rake and the broom and place them at the back of the chair, for if the witch has not the oven rake and broom with her, no one will know she is a witch. They also bind to her apron strings a muddy cow horn filled with magic oil, such as witches use when they ride to *Blåkulla*, the Witches' Kitchen. In the horn they stick a long feather, and, last, they hang an old post bag round her neck.

Then the maids go into the kitchen, and the housekeeper

comes up to the nursery to tell us children that one of those horrid witches who ride on a broomstick every Easter Eve has dropped down in the yard at Mårbacka. "She is sitting just outside the entrance," says the housekeeper, "and a hideous-looking creature she is! So you children had better stay in the house until she's gone."

But we know what is going to happen and rush past the housekeeper and down the steps to see the Easter witch. Papa of course comes with us, but Mamma and Aunt Lovisa say they prefer to remain inside, as they have seen so many Easter witches in their time.

Coming out on the porch to look for the witch, we see her sitting below, glaring up at us with her coal-black eyes. We pretend to be awfully frightened, and that we think she is really and truly a witch, on her way to the Blåkulla. We know, of course, that she is only a straw witch, but we are supposed to be frightened—that is part of the play. Otherwise, the maids who have gone to the trouble of making the effigy for us would have nothing for their pains. When we have gazed at the Easter witch awhile from a safe distance, we creep cautiously down the steps. She holds herself rigidly erect as we approach, until at last one of us thrusts a hand into the bag. The old, discarded post bag is bulging with mail, and we keep a watchful eye on it the whole time. But the one who is first to thrust a hand into the bag lets out a wild shriek of delight, for the bag is filled with letters.

We take out great handfuls of fat letters, all bearing seals, to each of which is attached a wing feather, as though they had flown hither. All the letters are for Johan and Anna and Gerda and me. The grownups get none.

As soon as we have gathered them up, we go into the house and sit down at the dining room table to open our Easter letters. It is heaps of fun, for Easter letters are seldom written with pen and ink but are painted. In the middle of the page of every letter stands a gay-colored Easter man or Easter woman holding a broom, a rake, a horn, and the other Pascal implements.

We receive many kinds of letters. Some are mere daubs done by small children, while others are in black ink like the usual letter, but always in the middle of the page stands the Old Easter Man or the Old Easter Woman done in colors. It is evident that the grownups have helped the children with some of the drawings; for they are not all done equally well, but we don't care. The important thing is to get many letters so we can boast about them when we go to church on Easter Sunday and meet our cousins from Gårdsjö.

As a matter of fact, it is not strictly true that there is no writing in these Easter letters, for some are covered with verse. We don't get much pleasure out of these verses, as they are merely old Easter rhymes which come year after year and which we already know by heart.

We always pretend to be surprised that the flying witch has brought us so many letters, although we expected them. We ourselves have devoted every spare moment, during the month of March, to drawing and painting, and have sent out our Easter letters to every manor house in this part of the country. So we know they have worked in the same way at the other manor houses and that the letters the Easter witch has brought have come from Gårdsjö, from Herrestad, from Visteberg and other manors.

When we have gone over our letters and figured out who has sent them, we remember the Easter witch and run out to the porch to have another look at her.

But now the chair is vacant; the witch has flown and taken the oven rake and broom with her. She must have been in a hurry to get to the Witches' Kitchen and flown off as soon as she had delivered the Easter post.

"It is lucky for her that she escaped," we say with a laugh, "for here comes Per of Berlin![1] Per is a Finn with hunter's blood in his veins." He has just stepped out of the office, where he has loaded two of Papa's shotguns. Taking his stand on the flagstone in front of the office, he fires the shots into the air. We know, of course, that he's shooting at the

[1]Lieutenant Lagerlöf named workmen's cottages after principal cities in Europe, as noted in "The Land of Heart's Desire" (page 157).

Easter witches although we cannot see them. But Per of Berlin, being a Finn, sees more than the rest of us and must know what he is doing.

This year we have painted many more Easter letters than usual. Elin Laurell is not so strict about our lessons as Aline used to be, therefore we have had more time to ourselves. The nursery at Mårbacka has been turned into a regular workshop with colors and mixing cups all over the room. The busiest time was during Holy Week, when Elin was in Karlstad visiting relatives. Papa was in despair because we had begged from him all his fine white linen paper. Finally he said that we'd have to be satisfied now with common yellow straw paper, as that was all he had left. The pretty red and blue colors with which we all love to paint had given out; so we had to run down to Aunt Lovisa and borrow the box of fine colors she had saved from her boarding school days at Åmål. All the drinking glasses in the nursery were taken to wash our brushes in, and we used up every stick of sealing wax in the house. Mamma sat addressing letters days on end, and we ran about in every lane searching for pretty feathers to attach to the envelopes with a seal. There was always a dearth of brushes, and when the last letter had been sealed, nothing was left of them but a few thin wisps of hair.

We are so glad that Easter Eve has come at last and we are through with the painting! If we receive as many letters in return as we sent out, it will take more than one Easter witch to deliver them.

In the late afternoon the housekeeper comes again to tell us that another dreadful witch is sitting below the porch, and to warn us children to stay indoors until she has gone. But we run down from the nursery at once to look at her. Papa, as usual, goes with us, and, for a change, Mamma and Aunt Lovisa come, too, and even Uncle Wachenfeldt, who is spending the Easter holidays with us, comes limping out to the porch.

It is cold outside, and windy; so the Easter witch can't have had any too pleasant a journey. We pretend, as usual, that we are afraid of her and steal down the steps softly and with the utmost caution.

This Easter witch is exactly like the other one; so we are not really and truly frightened at the sight of her, though we pretend to be. The straw sticks out below the sleeves of the jacket as on all Easter witches. The eyes, nose, and mouth, and two or three wisps of hair have been sketched with charcoal on a gray kitchen towel; the dairymaid's shawl is spread across the shoulders; the old, soiled post bag hangs round the neck, and tied to the apron strings is the filthy cow horn.

This time I am the first to thrust my hand into the post bag, but I have barely touched the letters when the sorceress jumps up. She quickly takes out the feather from the cow horn and smears my face with the witches' salve.

But how can this be? What does it mean? I cry out in terror as I rush toward the porch. But the straw woman can run, too, and is after me, hotfoot, to smear me again with the witches' oil.

Not only am I frightened, but I am also baffled by the strange sight of an Easter witch who can move. When she sprang up from the chair, anxious and perplexing thoughts ran through my mind. If an old stuffed sack can come to life, the dead, too, can rise from their graves, and wicked trolls are to be found in the woods. Then there is nothing too horrible or too uncanny to be true.

I run shrieking up the steps to the veranda. If I can only get to where the grown folks are, they will protect me. Anna, Gerda, and Johan rush past me in the same direction. They are as frightened as I am. But the grownups are standing on the porch, laughing.

"Dear children," they say, "there's nothing to be afraid of—it's only Nurse Maja!"

Then we understand, of course, how stupid we have been. We might have known it was Nurse Maja dressed up as an Easter witch. How provoking that we have let ourselves be so scared! And, most of all, it is provoking to one who, for several years, has practiced at being brave.

But this is no time to stand here blaming ourselves or

others; for now the Easter witch, with arms outstretched, comes rushing up the steps, making straight for Uncle Wachenfeldt to embrace and kiss him. And Uncle Wachenfeldt, who abhors all ugly women, spits and curses and fends her off with his cane. But I'm not so sure that he escapes her onslaught, for there are two black smudges on his white mustache.

The Easter witch, not content with that, gives him a poke with the oven rake and then rides off toward the kitchen. The pigeons, which are so tame they eat out of your hand and are not easily scared, take to their wings at sight of her, and the cat leaps onto the eaves trough, while Nero, the dog who is big as a bear, slinks out of her way with his tail between his legs. But the old housekeeper is not afraid. Quick as a flash, she runs over to the stove, seizes the steaming coffee pot, and goes straight up to the ogress the moment she appears on the threshold.

And when the Easter witch sees the raised coffee pot, she turns and flees in the direction of the barnyard, riding like mad on her broomstick. The first to see her is the old bay mare. She has just been unharnessed and is walking calmly toward the door of the stable, when the face of a scarecrow looms up before her. Without stopping to reflect, she doubles her legs against her belly and sets off, her mane flying, her tail standing out, her hoofs beating the earth—running wild till her way is barred by a high fence.

Lars of London and Magnus of Vienna, who are down by the shed cutting firewood, pause in their work when they see her. It would not do for sturdy fellows like them to flee at sight of a witch. Without moving from the spot, they raise their axes against her, knowing that witches are afraid of steel. Nor does the Easter witch dare to approach them.

Just then she sees a man coming down the avenue. Strangely enough, the man is Olle of Maggebysäter, who once in his youth came upon a band of Easter witches. While going home from a party one Easter Eve, on a meadow below Mårbacka, he saw them sweep across the field in a long procession. They wound themselves around him, like a snare.

Then they danced with him all night, over a newly plowed field, never letting him stop for a moment to take breath. He had thought then the witches would dance the life out of him, and now, as he comes to the servants' hall at Mårbacka, he sees just such a witch, as he had seen in his youth, come riding toward him on a broomstick.

He does not wait for her to come very close. Old and crippled with rheumatism as he is, he turns abruptly and runs down the avenue as swiftly as a boy, never stopping until he has reached the woods on the other side of the road.

Now that we children are over our fright, we can laugh as we follow at the heels of the Easter witch. We have seen the housekeeper threaten with steaming hot coffee; seen the horse shy, and Olle of Maggebysäter take to the woods. We have also seen Lars of London and Magnus of Vienna raise their axes at her. I don't think we have ever laughed so much in our lives!

The best of all is when Per of Berlin comes running past the porch toward the office. Papa asks him where he is hurrying to. The old man scarcely answers, but at last it comes out, he is going to load the shotguns again and shoot dead the horrible creature who runs about in the yard. Anyone can see that the zest of the chase is in his eyes. For old Per of Berlin has been gunning for Easter witches these fifty years and has never caught a single one. But here at last is a witch he can catch on the run.

THE BALL AT SUNNE

We are thankful that we live in East Ämtervik and not in Sunne. There are more people in Sunne, but they are not so jolly as the East Ämtervik folk. They never have any festivities; they have no brass sextet and no male quartet, and there are not so many who can make a speech or write a poem as there are at East Ämtervik.

The only interest we have in common is the dean. As the pastorate is a large one, the dean cannot invite all the families at the same time; so he usually asks those who live in East and West Ämtervik and Gräsmark at one time, and those who live in Sunne at another time.

In other respects, we have no contact with the Sunne folk. We never meet any of the leading families of Sunne, but we feel instinctively that they consider themselves above us because they live in a larger parish.

Once a year we are invited to a party at the deanery, but we do not meet any of the native sons there. Although we are not acquainted with the first families of Sunne, we have seen them all at the Ämbergshed fair, and know them by sight: the Squire Pettersons of Stöpafors, the Engineer Maules of Sundberg, the Engineer Igneliuses of Ulvsberg, the Squire Hellstedts of Skarped, and Squire Jonsson's family, who live at the "Castle" of Sundsvik.

On the seventeenth of August, many young men from Sunne come to Mårbacka to dance and to join in the festivities. They must have told the Sunneites that Hilda Wallroth of Gårdsjö and Anna Lagerlöf of Mårbacka have grown up to be the prettiest girls in the whole Fryken valley. At all events, one fine day Papa received a letter from two gentlemen of Sunne requesting the presence of himself and family at a buffet supper dance.

The dance was to be held in the rooms over Nilsson's general store, which they were to have, rent free, for the evening. The gentlemen were to furnish the beverages and the ladies were to bring coffee, tea, and cakes, or whatever else needed for the supper. It was to be a most unpretentious affair; the only outlay would be a few riksdalers for lights and gratuities.

A similar letter was sent to Gårdsjö, and Aunt Augusta came over to consult with Mamma and Aunt Lovisa as to what they should contribute, for they were not going to be outdone by the Sunne folk. Aunt Lovisa immediately set the dough for a big bake of fancy bread and cake. They used to have these buffet supper dances when Auntie was young. Not for a moment did she think of going to the ball; she knew very well that she was too old to dance, but she thought it nice there was something jolly to look forward to. It was the same with Gerda and me—we, too, thought it jolly that there was to be a dance, although we were too young to attend.

The day before the dance, as we sat at the dinner table talking about the ball, Papa said, "I think Selma is big enough now to go along with the others."

Papa thought I should be delighted to go to a dance, but indeed I was not. I had been to so many parties in East Ämtervik that I knew well enough how I would fare at the dance in Sunne! "I don't want to go," I promptly answered.

"Why don't you want to go to the ball?" Papa asked me. Then, turning to Mamma, he said, "Has she no dress?"

"Oh, yes," said Mamma. "She has her light gray cashmere dress, which will do well enough."

"How about the proper shoes and stockings?"

"Anna has outgrown the gray cloth shoes she wore at Sister Julia's wedding, and Selma can have those."

"Then," said Papa, "I see no reason why she shouldn't go."

I was seized with dread. I did not know of what I was afraid, but I could imagine no worse calamity than having to go to that Sunne ball!

"But, Papa, I am too young to go to a ball. I'm only thirteen."

"Emilia Wallroth is going," said Auntie, "and she is no older than you are."

56

When I saw that they were all against me—not only Papa and Mamma, but even Aunt Lovisa—I began to cry.

"My dear child," said Papa, "why do you cry when you are going to have a good time?"

"But I won't have a good time," I whimpered. "No one will dance with me because I am lame."

I was not angry, for ever since the day I played cards with Uncle Wachenfeldt I have kept my temper under control. And Papa wasn't angry, either; only he thought me a strange child.

"But Papa, you do not know how it feels when all the other girls are invited to dance and you are not. Or when you are asked for just a reel, or by some man no other girl would dance with."

"What nonsense!" said Papa, and his voice sounded terribly stern. "I want my daughters to go to a dance whenever it is possible."

"Gustaf, I think you might let her wait at least until she is fifteen," said Aunt Lovisa, coming to my aid rather late. It would have been better if she had not mentioned Emilia a moment ago.

Why, to be sure she may wait," said Papa. "But who knows whether there will be another ball in Sunne then? This is the first one they've had in many years."

I know that Papa hates to see us weep, and that he would be far more likely to let me off if I laughed and looked pleasant. But now I can't stop crying; the tears pour down my cheeks all through the dinner.

And I continue to weep while taking my noonday rest and during the afternoon lessons and while we are out tobogganing, and even when we sit at the round table in the dining room, working. Gerda usually cries a lot when she doesn't know her lessons, but I don't think she has ever kept it up from noon until bedtime.

When Mamma comes to the nursery to hear our evening prayers, I choke back the tears long enough to say an "Our Father" and "Lord Bless Us," but I stick at "God Who Cares for Little Children," and "An Angel Watches Over Us."

"Is it only on account of the ball you are crying?" Mamma queries. "Or is there some other reason?"

"Mamma, won't you please ask Papa if I may be excused from going to the dance?"

"Dear child, you know that Papa is only thinking of your pleasure."

"Yes, but I won't be asked to dance, and you know it, Mamma."

"Why, of course you will dance," says Mamma and goes her way.

My first thought on awaking next morning is: "This is the day of the ball," and straightaway I fall to weeping again. I did not know the eyes could shed so many tears; there seem to be no end to them!

Anna and Gerda are talking about the ball—who is to open it, and who is to have the first waltz with Anna, and whether Frökens Maule will dress in white. Anna has done up her hair in curl papers and hopes her curls will stay in until the ball is over. The more they talk of these things, the harder I cry. If I could only stop crying!

"Selma, you mustn't take on so," says Anna. "Your eyes will be red and swollen tonight if you cry like that." I promise not to weep any more, but I can't stop.

Anna, Mamma, and Elin Laurell are busy with their toilettes the whole forenoon. They baste ribbons on their frocks; iron their starched petticoats, and try on their shoes, for they want to look as attractive as possible. Aunt Lovisa thinks it strange that one should go to a ball in high-neck and long sleeves; it was not the correct thing when she was young. But Mamma says that Anna and I are only children, our party dresses will do well enough.

Later in the forenoon, I step into the dining room to see Papa. I find him seated in the rocker, as usual, reading the *Värmland News*. I walk straight up to him and place one foot on the rocker and one hand on his shoulder.

"What is it now?" he asks, turning to me.

"Papa, may I be excused from going to the ball?" I beg sweetly, for it has occurred to me that, by asking in all humility, I can persuade him to let me off. I also intend to remind him that it was on his account I read the Bible and, considering what I did for him, he ought to let me stay at home.

"You know, Papa, that I shall not be invited to dance, as I'm so lame that no one will dance with me." That is as far as I get when I burst into tears again.

Without a word, Papa rises from his chair and, taking me by the hand, leads me out to the kitchen. He asks the housekeeper to make me a nice thick sandwich with plenty of cheese on top, and goes his way.

Now I know that he will insist on my going to the ball. I feel like throwing the sandwich on the floor; but I dare not give way to my temper, or the wild beast in me will break loose again.

I conduct myself properly in every way, but I continue to cry. I weep at the dinner table; I weep afterward; I weep when we dress for the ball. In fact, I weep all the time until we are seated in the sleigh and the robes are tucked around us.

Then, at last, the tears must have known that nothing was gained by falling. As we drive into Sunne I sit in the sleigh—dry-eyed. I am wearing my gray cashmere dress with the blue border and Anna's light gray cloth shoes with the red silk laces. At the throat I have a pretty bright red rosette, which was a Christmas present from Uncle Kalle (he always gives us such dainty things for Christmas). Aunt Lovisa has dressed my hair so that it lies smooth and even, and twisted it into a big knot at the nape of the neck.

But what does it matter how I am dressed since my face is covered with blotches, and my eyes are red and swollen from weeping! I look so hideous that no one would ask me to dance, even if I did not limp.

There is a reception room opening into the ballroom, and as we come in the Wallroth girls tell us the Frökens Maule are dressing; that they are going to wear sheer white frocks, and, to keep their skirts from wrinkling, two maids carried them to Sunne on hangers suspended from a pole, and we all think it a grand idea.

"Oh, they can do that who have only a short distance to go!" says Anna.

Anna and Hilda are such pretty girls that no matter how the others may deck themselves out, they can never look so beautiful as these two girls. When the Frökens Maule come in I must admit that their dresses are lovely, and the girls are pretty, too, but they can't hold a candle to Anna and Hilda for beauty!

Emilia Wallroth is not at all good looking, but everyone says she has charm. Emilia is engaged for every dance. Nobody thinks of her plainness; for she is so lively and entertaining that every man would dance with her, even if she were lame.

The reception room is now crowded with matrons and girls. The music strikes up, so everyone must be here. It is the brass sextet from East Ämtervik that is playing, for they have no musicians in Sunne. Squire Vilhelm Stenbäck of Björsbyholm comes into the reception room. He says, "Since there has been no ball in Sunne for, at least, twenty years, I propose that we open this festal occasion with a promenade polonaise, as is customary at state balls."

Then the elderly gentlemen come into the reception room and offer an arm to the elderly ladies—Fru Maule, Fru Hellstedt, Fru Pettersson, Fru Bergman, Fru Wallroth, and Fru Lagerlöf, and they go into the ballroom arm in arm. The young gentlemen now come in and ask the young ladies for the opening dance. There is no one left in the reception room but old Mamselle Eriksson of Skäggeberg and me. And Mamselle Eriksson is at least fifty years old and has thin yellow braids coiled around her ears and long yellow teeth.

There is a gentleman here we haven't seen before. He is in uniform and is said to be the inspector of Kil railway station. He is a stranger, apparently, and when he comes into the reception room to look for a dancing partner, and finds no one but Mamselle Eriksson and me, I wonder which one he will choose. But he turns away at once without taking either of us. Here we sit—Mamselle Eriksson and I—motionless and silent. But all the same I am glad she is here so that I am not left all alone.

I think it is just as well that no one asks me to dance, for now Papa will know that it is the truth that nobody wants to dance with me. It is small consolation, however, for I am having a dreary time.

I wonder who could have induced Mamselle Eriksson of Skäggeberg to come to the ball. For surely she did not come of her own accord!

When the promenade polonaise is over and the dancers return to the reception room, both young and old are in gay spirits. Mamma sits down on the sofa, between Fru Maule and Fru Hellstedt, and they laugh and chat as if they were old friends. Anna sits down by the side of Hilda Ignelius, and whispers to her, and Hilda Wallroth comes in, arm in arm, with Julia Maule.

Afterward there are waltzes, polkas, and reels, waltzes, polkas, and reels—over and over again. Anna and Hilda and Emilia, of course, are in demand for every dance. They are full of life and merriment. Hilda comes over to me and suggests that I go into the ballroom with them and watch the other dancers.

But that I don't wish to do. How to avoid it, I do not know; but Anna quickly comes to the rescue: "You'd better not talk to Selma, or she might start crying again."

After the promenade polonaise Mamma and the other matrons dance no more, but they go back to the ballroom to watch the young folks dance. Once more the reception room is entirely deserted, save for me and Mamselle Eriksson. We two remain in our seats the whole evening.

I try to think of all the people who are more unfortunate than I am: the sick, the poor, the blind. Why should you grieve because you are not asked to dance at a ball? What if you were blind?

I wonder whether this is punishment for something I have said or done, or if it is a lesson in humility. I remember the story of Mamselle Brorström that Papa used to tell; of how some students at the gymnasium in Karlstad invited her to the Market Fair Ball and let her sit there alone the whole evening. She must have thought it strange that she was so unattractive that no one would dance with her, for that is just what I am thinking of myself now.

Next morning, at the breakfast table, Mamma, Elin Laurell, Emma, and Anna tell Papa of the good time they had at the ball last night, and how well everything went off. I say nothing, for I have nothing to say. When Anna has named all with whom she had danced, Papa asks how Selma fared.

"Selma wasn't asked to dance," Mamma replies. She is too young, you know."

Papa sits musing a while. Then he says: "Don't you think, Louise, that we should write to Stockholm to see if the Afzeliuses can take Selma another winter and let her attend the Institute? She improved so much the last time she was there. I should like to see her well and strong before I die."

My eyes nearly pop out of my head. Perhaps Papa feels conscience-stricken because he made me go to the ball last night? Perhaps that is why he wants to send me to Stockholm?

There's no one so nice as my Papa!

THE POND

Although I am now thirteen years old, I remember well the old duck pond we had at Mårbacka when we were little.

It was a small round pond. In summer it was black with tadpoles, and in the autumn it was covered with a green scum which, happily, hid the tadpoles from sight. The water in the pond was so muddy that it could not be used for washing clothes. Nor could one bathe in it on account of the quantities of horse leeches that abounded there. If a person were to get one of these horse leeches on him, it would not let go until it had sucked all the blood out of his body. The housekeeper says they are more dangerous than the big leeches she keeps in a water bottle on the kitchen windowsill to draw out the blood from a swollen cheek caused by an aching tooth.

I remember that we had small joy of that pond while open, but when it froze over, in the late autumn, it was another matter. The morning that Nurse Maja informed us that the ice was firm, we hardly took time to get into our clothes before we were off. Papa went with us in order to test the ice with his cane, to make sure it was solid. We brought down from the garret all our old skates and ran over to the stableman to have him grind them and put new straps where they were needed.

We were awfully keen about skating when we were little, and the fact that we had only a small pond to skate on didn't trouble us in the least. Toward Christmas, when the snow began to fall, we had a lot of bother keeping the ice clear. We shoveled and swept until the thirteen-day blizzard, when we had to give up skating and take to coasting instead.

Sometimes folks would say to Papa they thought it strange that he, who was such a lover of beauty, did not ditch out the duck pond. It was of no use to anyone, they said, and might even be a menace to health because of the horrible stench that arose from there on hot summer days. And, besides, it lay close to the road, in plain sight of everyone who came to Mårbacka. Even Aunt Lovisa, who otherwise clung faithfully to everything old, told Papa, time and time again, that the pond spoiled the looks of the whole place.

Whenever there was mention of doing away with the duck pond, we children became dreadfully alarmed. For we didn't mind the tadpoles in spring or the stale odor in summer; we thought only of the skating. I must say there were not so many pleasures one could have in November and December; so we really needed the pond to skate on.

It was a long time before Papa did anything about the duck pond. He built the new barn and laid out the new garden, but the pond remained unchanged. We children naturally thought it was for our sakes that he refrained from ditching out the pond, for we were the only ones who had any joy of it.

Then came a summer when Sven of Paris and Magnus of Vienna began to work down by the duck pond; so we understood that Papa had been obliged to yield to the wishes of Aunt Lovisa and the others who wanted to be rid of it.

Still we couldn't make out just what Sven of Paris and Magnus of Vienna were doing. They had hauled stone and gravel with which they were building a wall—not right around the duck pond, but at a short distance from it. What on earth was that wall for, we wondered.

At all events it became clear to us that there would be no more skating. I remember that we children said among ourselves that it was awfully mean of Aunt Lovisa to make Papa do away with the pond, and that Papa didn't care so much for us as we thought, or he wouldn't have had the heart to deprive us of our greatest pleasure.

We asked Sven of Paris and Magnus of Vienna why they were putting up the wall, and they said that it was being built for the purpose of doing away with the old mud hole which held nothing but frogs and horse leeches.

We could hardly look at the wall, but despite our prayers,

64

it grew from day to day, till at last it was finished. Then Sven of Paris and Magnus of Vienna cleared away the sod around the pond, and when that was done, they were ready to begin the ditching.

One morning, as we got out of bed, we saw all the grownups—Papa, Mamma, Aunt Lovisa, Uncle Schenson, and the housekeeper—go down to the duck pond. We knew then that the ditching was about to begin. We were so furious with the whole proceeding that we wouldn't even look at what they were doing. But curiosity must have got the upper hand, for it wasn't long before we, like the others, stood down by the duck pond, looking on.

We had come at just the right moment. On the south side of the pond stood Sven and Magnus in their bare feet, their trousers rolled above their knees, and their spades raised to cut through the bank of the pond. Papa gave the order: "One, two, three—go!" With that, the ditching began. The spades flashed as the men heaved the earth to one side, and water from the pond came rushing out into a narrow trench.

It gushed out merrily, bubbling and purling. We thought the water looked jubilant over its release. If it had only known that this was the end of the old duck pond, we said, perhaps it would not have run off with such glee.

It flowed rapidly over the ground to the south of the pond, where the turf had been removed, filling every hollow, and making a detour around each stone in its path, forcing its way farther and farther from the pond, pausing at times as if exhausted, until reinforcements coming from the pond sent it onward again until it reached the gravel embankment, where it suddenly stopped. As it could advance no farther, it spread below the wall.

Sven of Paris and Magnus of Vienna dug and dug, and the water came pouring from the pond faster and faster, until the water itself did the work without their having to dig further. Just as through a dish with a hole in one side, the water flowed through the southern bank, forming many small rivulets that found their way to the wall, there to spread themselves out.

But after a while the water flowed more slowly; it collected in small pools and stood in puddles. To us children it looked as though the water was no longer so eager to escape from its old home. Then Sven of Paris and Magnus of Vienna dug a hole in the eastern bank. After that the water flowed faster. We had never imagined there was so much water in the old duck pond! It spread both to south and east, covering an area three times as large as that of the old duck pond.

Oh, but we children were stupid! There we stood, grieving and angry because our old pond would be no more. But at last we saw that instead of the pond being drained, it had become many times larger than it was before. If the pond was to be as big as that, we would have a great place to skate on. We actually turned giddy at the thought of it.

We saw and marveled, but we could not express our delight until we were quite sure the pond was not being drained. Imagine our joy when we heard Papa say that he had decided it was better to widen the pond than to do away with it entirely! The water would be clearer and better when the pond had been enlarged. It could be used for washing clothes, and, in case of fire, we would have a pond large enough to fetch water from.

And all the grownups congratulated Papa on this great improvement. Though neither Papa nor the others mentioned the improved skating pond, we children felt that he had done this for us so that we would have more room to whirl about.

In the late summer, when the Hammargrens, the Afzeliuses, Fru Hedberg, Uncle Kristofer, and Aunt Julia came to Mårbacka, they were astonished to see the new lake in place of the old duck pond. And every morning Papa took Uncle Hammargren and Uncle Oriel, Uncle Schenson and Uncle Kristofer down to the pond to show them what he had done. Here he had cut a hole through the wall for a drain and put up a sluice gate so that too much water would not escape. Then he took them up to the place where he had dug a canal to convey the water from the woods.

They thought it had all been admirably planned and

executed, but what they admired most was the great culvert Papa had lain under the road for the water to flow through into the lake. I don't think Papa ever received so much praise for anything he had done as for this ditching.

One evening when Uncle Schenson and Fru Hedberg returned from a walk in the twilight, they told of a strange light they had seen hovering over the pond. It was not moonlight, for the moon had not yet risen, nor was it a reflection of the sunset, for that evening the sun had been under a cloud. Supper was on the table, but Mamma and all the guests—and Papa, too, of course—rushed out to the pond to see the strange shimmer.

Coming back, some said it was probably a tin of anchovies that lay shining at the bottom of the pond, others thought it must be phosphorescent wood which had been thrown into the water, but Fru Hedberg would not accept these conjectures. She said that which she had seen was a bluish phosphorescence rising from the water, and that there was something mystical and supernatural about it.

We children were down by the pond also, but we saw nothing remarkable, and we were inclined to believe it was something Fru Hedberg had imagined. But the mysterious light afforded the grownups much pleasure. Every evening they marched down to the pond in solemn procession to see the phosphorescent light rise from the water. And it created no end of controversy. Finally Uncle Oriel proposed that we call the new lake "Phosphoresque," to which they all agreed.

But the marvelous light that appeared every night on Mårbacka Lake became the talk of the whole countryside, and when the seventeenth of August came round again and Sexton Melanoz was to write his customary lyric in honor of Papa's anniversary, the pond figured largely in the birthday verses.

It was a long poem and was sung to the tune of "I Remember Those Blessed Days," by Fru Lenngren. The brothers Schullström and Herr Gustaf Asker and Fru Jacobson, a sister of the brothers Schullström, sang the verses lustily and well. All I can remember of the poem are the lines about the pond:

> *And this love of beauty*
> *That made of a fen a lake,*
> *Which to future generations*
> *Will be known as Phosphoresque.*

I do not recall that anything out of the ordinary happened to the pond that year. But the following spring, Nurse Maja came up to the nursery one morning and told us that Mårbacka Lake had disappeared and that now the old duck pond was back again. That was all she would say. When we got dressed, we could go and see for ourselves.

Naturally we had prided ourselves on having a lake at Mårbacka, like the one at Gårdsjö and at Herrestad. So we hurriedly put on our clothes and ran out. Then we saw with our own eyes that Nurse Maja had told the truth.

We were having our worst spring rains just then. The previous day the ice had broken up in Mårbacka Lake, and a magnificent sight it was. When the lake had cast off its coverlet of ice, the water rose to the edge of its banks, and quantities of water came rushing down.

But in the night, it had rained so hard and the pond had become so full of water that it washed away the whole wall that Sven and Magnus had put up the previous summer. We were aghast when we saw the havoc the storm had wrought. It had torn away large stones and hurled them far out in the meadow, and had thrown the gravel even farther away. The willow slips that Papa had planted on top of the embankment were now on their way down to Lake Fryken.

Here was the abomination of desolation! The entire area where the water had risen so proudly the day before now lay waste. There was nothing left of the beautiful lake but soft clay with here and there a puddle of water. The old duck pond, however, had not been disturbed.

There it lay, nestling securely in its bed—a small round body of water—no larger, no smaller than it had been before.

We thought, as we looked at it, that it smiled with mischievous glee, as if proclaiming it had come into its own again.

But Papa couldn't let the pond remain as it was of old. He had received more praise for this work of improvement than for any of his other undertakings. Hadn't the sexton written a poem about it? Hadn't all the relatives been keenly interested? And hadn't Fru Hedberg seen that marvelous blue shimmer hovering over the waters of the pond? The reputation of the whole property was at stake.

Although they were busy with the spring work, Papa could not rest until the wall had been rebuilt. The men had to haul stone and gravel down to the pond and do masonry work instead of harrowing and sowing. Lars of London and Magnus of Vienna shook their heads in dismay at these orders. Per, being a Finn, understood the mysteries of water. He said right out that all this labor was useless. Something that lived in the old duck pond wanted it left the way it had been from time immemorial.

However, the wall was put up and covered, not only with gravel like the former one, but with sod. And two rows of willow slips were planted on the wall, which were to send their roots down between the stones, to help hold them together. It was a good job, and after a few heavy showers, the lake was again filled with water. When in August the guests arrived, Mårbacka Lake lay there, glimmering and shining just as it had the previous summer. The only difference was that Fru Hedberg's blue phosphorescence was not to be seen on the surface of the water; it must have been washed away by the devastating storms of the spring.

The following year, Papa took special precautions during the breaking up of the ice. Every day he examined the wall, inch by inch, for cracks through which water could seep. If he found so much as a drop of water leaking out, he had his workmen strengthen the wall with more stones, mortar, and gravel. If it rained in the night, Papa arose and went down to the pond to be on hand in case anything should happen.

The whole house was always in a state of unrest on account of that pond! No one had any peace of mind until the spring rains were over. Cracks in the wall occurred regularly every spring and the wall had to be mended or braced continually, but it was not washed away until the year that Papa came home with inflammation of the lungs from sleeping between damp sheets.

Mamma had no time to think of the pond or to have the cracks in the wall stopped. The breaking of the ice came early that spring, and by Easter everything went wrong. The stableman came in on Easter Eve to tell us that the water had begun to force its way under the wall. Mamma said it was too bad, but he must try to find someone to help him. But that was impossible. It was Easter Sunday, and the workmen in all the cottages had brought home brandy, and they wouldn't bother about the lake. Anyhow, the lake was man-made, they said, and had been on the place only a couple of years.

And so on Easter Sunday the water was allowed to work all the damage it could, and by Monday morning the entire wall had collapsed and lay scattered over the meadows, while the whole lake bottom was exposed - except the old duck pond. That lay securely within its banks, round as ever, and twinkled and gleamed as if happy at being again master of all it surveyed.

Papa, who was well enough now to sit up, was informed that the wall had broken down a second time. He became so disheartened that we feared he would have a relapse. But the first thing he did when he was able to take hold of things himself was to raise the wall for the third time.

He was not very happy at having to rebuild the wall once more. There was all the spring work to be done, and the farm laborers were tired of the everlasting bother with the pond, which was of no earthly use to anyone. But there was nothing to do but rebuild, since Papa insisted that the honor of his estate demanded that Mårbacka Lake should be restored. Considering all the praise showered upon him, he couldn't revert to the old duck pond.

While the workmen were rebuilding the wall, Uncle Wachenfeldt came driving down to Mårbacka in his little carriole. He had heard that Papa was ill and had come to see how it was with him. When he saw the men at work on the new wall, he drew rein and shook his head. Then, as he drove toward the house, he said to Papa, "If you put up your wall in that way, Erik Gustaf, you will have to rebuild it every year."

"You don't say so, Wachenfeldt! Now you're very clever. I wish you would tell me of a better way."

"Don't fill it in with loose gravel if you want the wall to hold, but put the gravel into sacks as they do in war time when building a trench."

Papa followed his advice, and from that time to this the wall has stood, for which we are all thankful. Every spring it had been a source of anxiety to us, as each day we expected to hear that the wall had collapsed again.

Shortly after Papa had built a wall that would hold, he went to Strömstad. While down by the sea, he must have thought of his lake and have seen what it lacked by comparing it with Kattegat. At all events, he had no sooner returned than he undertook further improvements.

He again planted a row of willows on either side of the wall and laid a graveled walk between them so the folks would have a shore promenade like the one at Laholmen in Strömstad. And he said that when the willows were grown, he would build a pavilion at the southeast corner of the wall from which the view was loveliest. And in his old age, he would sit in the pavilion in August when the harvest moon was full and see the trees, which he had planted, mirrored in the waters of the lake.

The willows grew and flourished, but everything else that Papa tried to do to beautify the pond failed. Poor Papa! I felt so sorry for him.

In the summer, when Daniel and Johan were at home, Daniel helped Aunt Lovisa with the flowers. He loved to work in the garden, hoeing and weeding like a regular gardener. Aunt Lovisa was glad of the help he gave her, but Johan, on the contrary, had a bent for mechanics.

When Papa got back from Strömstad, Johan suggested

71

that he let him build a craft of some sort to sail the pond. As Papa had been out sailing every day at Strömstad, he thought that if Mårbacka Lake only had boats, it wouldn't be so far behind Kattegat; so he promised at once to let the boy try.

Johan made a small raft about eight feet square and nailed an empty ale keg under each corner so that it could carry a heavy cargo without sinking. Then he made an engine out of an old spinning wheel and an oven rake—the rake to go underneath the boat and the wheel above. Johan was to stand behind the wheel and steer. The moment he turned the wheel, the propeller under the water would begin to work and the boat would skim across the lake from shore to shore.

We were elated over Johan's invention. Now, we thought, he would be able to sail the pond, and we wondered if he might not be another John Ericsson, but we were wrong. When he turned the spinning wheel, the boat did not move. So that hope was dashed.

But there was much else that moved on the waters at Strömstad besides boats and ships. There were also wild ducks and eider ducks. Papa decided he would have waterfowl, too, so he wrote to some place in West Gothnia for geese. And one fine day, there came to Herrestad Pier seven goslings, which the stableman was ordered to fetch.

Everyone said they were fine geese. They were by no means small; on the contrary, they were nearly full grown. Aunt Lovisa said it was a pleasure to have geese on the place as in her parents' time, and the housekeeper told us about the gander that flew away with the wild geese one spring, when Fru Raklitz ruled at Mårbacka, and came back in the autumn with a mate and nine half-grown goslings. We were disappointed because the geese were not white, but the grownups said they were just as good as the white geese.

The geese were penned up in the cow barn for a week so that they would become accustomed to the place and not stray when we let them out. On the eighth day they were allowed to move about in the barnyard. And, indeed, they were tame and well behaved! They did not chase you or nip at your skirts, as geese generally do, but directly they were let out, they went over to the nearest meadow and began cropping grass, as if they were cows or sheep.

We children were eager to see the geese swim, but as the lake was at some distance from the cow barn, Papa thought they had better stay in the barnyard. In the morning, when they had become more accustomed to their surroundings, we might let them go swimming in Mårbacka Lake.

There is a small pond near the barn where the cows drink after grazing in the meadow, but we were so impatient to see the West Gothnia geese swim that we drove them to the little pond. We had always thought that geese would be so glad of the least little pool of water that they would dive in at once. But these geese simply would not go down to the byre pond. Then we said it must be because they were used to better things, that they would not go down into a dirty pond. It would be different in the morning when they could swim in nice clear water.

Next day we drove the geese to the big pond, but apparently the fine West Gothnia geese did not see how much better this was than the byre pond. They walked all around the banks of Mårbacka Lake, honking and nibbling grass, and did not even look at the water, much less stick their bills into it.

Uncle Schenson said that the West Gothnia geese had grown up on a farm where there was no open body of water, and, therefore, they had not learned to swim when they were goslings. They did not know they were waterfowl.

We tried to accustom them to the lake by throwing bread crumbs on the water, to make them swim out after the bread, but they only strove to get back on land. The geese were more afraid of water than were our turkeys.

I remember how all the boys and girls at Mårbacka once formed a half-circle round the geese and drove them down to the lake. When the geese reached the edge of the water and saw that there was no way of escape, they spread their small wings and flew in terror to the opposite shore—glad they had managed to save themselves from drowning.

So one could truthfully say that Papa had no luck with his attempts to beautify the place, and we really pitied him. But Papa was not one to give up so easily. He must have thought that, since he could not have boats and water birds floating on the surface of the lake, he would have better luck with things that live and move in the water.

So he made arrangements with some small boys who lived near Gårdsjö Lake to catch a lot of small fish for him. And every Sunday, when the boys were free from school, they came to Mårbacka carrying big bucketfuls of roach and perch which Papa emptied into the lake. Every day for a whole week we children stood out on the bank and cast bread crumbs to the fishes.

But it seemed strange that, although he had poured such great quantities of small fish into the pond every Sunday, we never saw them afterwards. They never appeared at the surface of the water and never bobbed up to catch gnats, as fishes usually do at dusk. They all disappeared at once, and yet they couldn't have died or they would have floated upon the surface.

"They must have escaped through the drain," said Papa. And he put up a grating at the mouth of the drain which would let the water flow through but not the fishes.

When the boys came again on Sunday, bringing their perch and roach, the grating had been put up. Now he knew the fish could not escape. But his joy was of short duration, for the following morning the pond was literally covered with tiny dead fish. It was a ghastly sight as they floated there, pale and bloated, their bellies exposed to the air. To think that just the previous evening they had been swimming about on their tiny fins, and now they were dead! It was enough to make the angels weep!

We children said among ourselves that Papa would have to give up his attempts, for now it was plain that no fish could live in our lake. But a few days later we heard Papa ask Sven of Paris if he, who had run about the woods all his life, did not know of some pool where carp were to be found.

Sven of Paris scratched his head and pondered a moment; then he said that when he was a small boy he and his father had once fished for carp in a pool far up among the Gårdsjö hills. "We did not catch them with hooks," he said, "but set out a trough in which we had spread some dough, and soon after we had lowered the trough into the water it was full of fish. They were fat carp and glittered like gold, but they weren't much good for eating. When we brought them home, Mother didn't want to prepare them. She said they tasted like clay, and she was right about it."

But the very next Sunday, Papa sent Sven of Paris up to the pools in the Gårdsjö hills to catch carp for him. Sven took with him a baking trough, a clump of dough, and a brass kettle to put the fish in. All this was done with the utmost secrecy. I don't think even Mamma or Aunt Lovisa knew on what sort of errand Sven had gone. Only we children knew.

We waited all day Sunday, but Sven did not appear. Perhaps he could not find the carp pool, we said, and had given up the search and gone home. On Monday Sven of Paris came, as usual, at five in the morning to help the milkmaid curry the cows and drive them out to pasture. But not a word did he say about carp.

When Papa had finished his breakfast, he went down to the barnyard, where he met Sven trundling a wheelbarrow. "Well, Sven," he said, "did you find the carp pool?"

"Sure I found it," said Sven of Paris, "but I had to tramp about in the woods all day Sunday."

"Did you catch any carp?"

"None worth talking about. Only small fry came to the bake trough to eat dough. The big fish must have been asleep at the bottom of the pool."

"So you thought it would not pay to bring the small fry home?"

"No. Sure they were nothing to carry home," said Sven of Paris.

"But what became of the brass kettle and the dough trough?"

"I put them in the servants' hall when I came back this

morning."

Papa must have felt as though he were being pursued by ill luck, but he took it with his usual calm. He gave Sven a riksdaler for his trouble and bade us children go over to the servants' hall for the brass kettle and dough trough and take them into the kitchen.

We found the brass kettle full of water, in which were a lot of tiny fishes, the smallest we had ever seen. We ran out to Papa as fast as we could and showed him the fish. He was delighted. They were genuine carp. Why Sven of Paris had not told him that he had the carp, no one knew. But, as Papa would say, Sven had his own way of doing things.

We dropped the fish into the lake. No one knew but Papa and us children that they were there. And Papa said we were not to tell anyone. "We must first see how the fish thrive," he told us.

As the grating was up before the outlet, there was no way for the young carp to escape, but we feared that they might meet the same fate as the perch and roach from Gårdsjö Lake. No carp, however, were seen to drift lifeless on the pond next morning. Twice a week Papa took us up to the storeroom and filled our aprons with grains of rye, which we cast on the water as food for the carp. We never saw any of them, and we were almost certain they had slipped away, but anyhow we did as Papa bade us.

Sometimes, when we sat down to dinner, Papa complained because there was only meat on the table day after day. "You must remember that Schenson comes from Karlstad," he would say to Aunt Lovisa. "And one who lives but a stone's throw from the Klar River is accustomed to having fish for his dinner."

Papa only said that because he himself preferred fish to meat, but the remark embarrassed Uncle Schenson; he was afraid Aunt Lovisa might think he was dissatisfied with the food served at Mårbacka, and hastened to turn the matter aside with a jest.

"We'll have to do without fish until we can take it out of Mårbacka Lake," he said.

That silenced Papa, for he did not want Aunt Lovisa or Uncle Schenson to know about the carp.

We continued to cast rye on the water until it began to freeze over. After it had frozen solid, Papa went out on the ice every day to see that there was an air hole in the ice, so that the carp could breathe.

When the winter was over and summer had come, we went again with Papa to the storeroom to have our aprons filled with rye to cast upon the waters of the lake. And we kept this up for several years without having seen so much as the tail of a fish. It was sinful, we thought, to throw away so much good rye uselessly, but we did it all the same.

To think that this is Papa's birthday—oh, what in the world shall we do! Jansson went down to the landing this morning to fetch the salmon that had been ordered from Karlstad, and he has just come back to tell us that there was no fish on the boat.

The housekeeper and Aunt Lovisa and Mamma, too, are almost frantic. They don't know what to do, and they will have to tell Papa, who is out on the porch with Uncle Schenson, how badly things have turned out.

"Here we're expecting a hundred guests to supper," said Aunt Lovisa, "and we have no salmon."

"Don't you think it would be advisable to send word to the Gårdsjö folk to bring a few pike along when they come?" Mamma suggests.

"I suppose that is the best we can do under the circumstances," Aunt Lovisa says. "But it's provoking, all the same, not to have anything better than a few half-starved pike to set before our guests."

"So it is," says Uncle Schenson. "This would be a fitting occasion to serve some fish from Mårbacka Lake."

When Papa hears that, he can't hold in any longer. Now, he thinks, is the proper time to reveal the secret.

"Don't be uneasy, Lovisa. There will be plenty of fish for supper, and we'll have it here in less than an hour."

With that he puts on his hat and goes out to find Daniel and Johan and bid them take a message to Pastor Lindegren, at Halla. We know that Pastor Lindegren loves to fish, and several times he has taken the boys with him on long fishing trips, but we don't see how he can help us out. He can't have put out any lines today, surely; so it isn't likely that he will have any fish before tomorrow morning, and by that time the birthday party will be over.

But in a moment we see Pastor Lindegren and the boys coming down the road. The boys are lugging a heavy net, and the pastor himself is carrying a long fishing rod over his shoulder. They are coming to the house, but stop first at the pond.

Then everyone rushes down to the pond—the home folk, the Hammargrens, the Afzeliuses, Fru Hedberg, and all the cousins who have come to to celebrate Papa's birthday. Pastor Lindegren stands out on the small washing bridge at the northeast end and lowers his fishing pole into the water. He moves it back and forth very carefully, but when he draws it up there is no fish on the hook.

"Just as we expected," the guests remark. What kind of fish did they expect to find in the pond? "Only frogs can live there," says Uncle Schenson.

But Pastor Lindegren does not give up. He unties the net while Daniel and Johan take off their heavy shoes and stockings and wade in, dragging the net along the banks of the pond to the opposite shore. Then, lowering the net, they drag it a short distance over the bed of the pond.

With that, there is life in the water. It bubbles as if it were boiling. A furious splashing is heard; then a swift rippled, and suddenly a big shining, yellow fish bobs up to the surface.

Pastor Lindegren is so excited he can hardly contain himself. He shouts an order to the boys to haul up the seine, and they quickly raise it to the surface. The net is full of glittering golden fish. It is as if they fished up nuggets of gold.

"What do you say now, Schenson?" asks Papa. "Don't you think these 'frogs' will make good eating?"

78

Pastor Lindegren stands there, looking radiant and proud, but the one who looks still more radiant is my father. Now he feels amply repaid for all the humiliation he has suffered and for all the cutting remarks he has endured. He receives again praise and congratulations as at the time when the pond was newly dredged and was called Lake Phosphoresque.

Aunt Nana Hammargren and Aunt Georgina Afzelius stand a little apart from the others, talking in undertones.

"I don't like this thing, Georgina," says Aunt Nana. "In former years when we came to Mårbaka, Gustaf was eager to show us the improvements he had made. He had extended his property by the purchase of adjacent land, or put up new buildings, or laid out gardens, or planted oak trees and Lombardy poplars. There was always something useful or beautiful for us to see, but all he thinks of now is that dreadful pond."

"Let me tell you, Nana, Louise is worried about Gustaf. She says he is far from well, that he has been ailing ever since he had that severe lung trouble three years ago."

"He has gone gray uncommonly fast," observes Aunt Nana thoughtfully.

"And he has fallen away also."

"But what does his illness have to do with the pond?"

"Well, you see, Louise believes that Gustaf is no longer able to undertake any regular work, but that he must have something to potter with, to make it appear that he is accomplishing something."

"My poor brother!" Aunt Nana says with a heavy sigh.

It is a pity that I should have heard this on Papa's birthday when we usually have such a jolly time! My heart aches for him—it hurts me so dreadfully! I shall feel this as long as I live.

THE WELL

We are sitting on the stoop at Mårbacka—everyone says we should call it veranda now, as "stoop" is so old-fashioned—hoping that Aunt Nana Hammargren will feel able to tell us a story this evening as she has done every evening since she came to Mårbacka. Aunt Nana has stayed a little longer than the other guests, that she might have a quiet visit with Mamma and Papa and Aunt Lovisa. We have had glorious weather while Aunt Nana has been here, so that we could sit outdoors until eleven o'clock in the evening. And she has sat on the steps with us children and told story after story.

Aunt Nana Hammargren has a lovely voice that brings the tears to our eyes when she tells of something beautiful. And Aunt Nana is beautiful herself, and happy, too, for she and Uncle Hammargren are a perfect match and very much in love with each other. We used to feel sorry for Aunt Nana because she has no daughters, only three sons, but she herself seems quite satisfied with what she has.

We children had counted on a story from Aunt Nana tonight also, but this morning she suddenly became ill. She was perfectly well before the post came and she began to read the *Värmland News*. She had no more than glanced at the paper when she said she had a severe headache and must go to her room and lie down.

I don't understand how one could get a headache from reading the *Värmland News*, for I have gone over it from the first page to the last and found nothing unusual. We have not seen Aunt Nana since, and fear there will be no story from her tonight.

But imagine our joy when Aunt Nana comes out on the porch and says she is better now. She sits down on the steps with us children; this time she tells us a true story that has been handed down.

80

It is nearly dark, but I can see that Aunt Nana is pale and her eyes are as red from weeping as mine were when I went to the ball in Sunne. But her voice was never more beautiful, and whatever she says, even the humorous things, somehow becomes strangely touching. I have to swallow hard to keep the tears from falling.

Aunt Nana's Story

This happened one summer when my parents were living. The housekeeper—the same Maja Persdotter who is here today—sat in the kitchen one morning pounding salt in a brass mortar, when a man came to the door and asked to see the Paymaster of the Regiment. The housekeeper replied that the Paymaster was not at home, which was the truth. The man then asked if he could speak to Fru Lagerlöf.

"She is sick," said the housekeeper, which was also the truth; for my mother had suffered from toothache all night and was lying down on the sofa in the room adjoining the kitchen with a hot poultice on her cheek.

She thought the stranger would leave when he heard that, but instead he strode over to the low settle, which stood below the table-bed then as now, and, seating himself, stretched out his long legs.

"I wonder if Fru Lagerlöf will be able to see me if I wait awhile?" he said.

The housekeeper wanted to know the nature of his business with her master and mistress. The stranger informed her that he was a well digger, and as he had heard that the water at Mårbacka was poor, he had come to dig a proper well. His name was Germund Germundsson, a name, he averred, that was known throughout all Värmland. He had dug wells on almost every manorial estate in the province, and everywhere he had brought forth good water, so he knew that the owners had cause to remember him with gratitude.

The housekeeper had never heard of the man and his great renown. Observing him more closely, she said to herself: "If the decision rested with me, he'd get no work from

81

my employers." The man was exceedingly tall and of powerful build, but his head was noticeably small and narrow at
the top. His eyes were dark and piercing, his nose stood out
like the beak of a bird of prey, and he had a strong, pugna-
cious chin. He was a person she wished to have out of the
house as quickly as possible.

"There have been many well diggers here, both in the
Paymaster's time and before it," she said. "They ran about
with willow branches searching for water veins on every hill,
but for all that, the drinking water here was no better."

"They must have been poor wretches who didn't know
their business," said the man. "But it's different with me.
You might at least let Fru Lagerlöf know that I'm here."

But that was exactly what the housekeeper did not
intend to do. She knew better than anyone else that the
water at Mårbacka was bad. There was only one well where
they had water the year around, even in the worst drought.
But the water was so turbid and brackish that it wasn't fit to
drink. Clear water had to be brought every day from a cold
spring that lay far from the house. But she would rather
carry drinking water any distance than have ought to do
with a tramp like Germund Germundsson.

"You needn't think you'll get me to call the mistress.
She's got an aching tooth. I've just been in and put a hot
poultice on her cheek, so I think she is sleeping now."

"Well, then," said the well digger, "there's nothing to do
but wait until she wakes up."

He crossed his long legs and leaned against the back of
the settle to make himself as comfortable as possible. The
housekeeper began to pound her mortar again. It was some
time before either of them spoke. But at last the well digger
broke the silence by asking her what she was pounding.

"Salt," she snapped.

"Oh, that is why your tongue is so dry!"

The housekeeper made no retort. She would not permit
herself to bandy words with a facetious stranger. There was
another interval of silence. Presently the kitchen door
opened and two maids came in with a big cowlful of water,

which they carried on a pole laid across their shoulders. It was a heavy burden, and their backs must have ached as they lowered the cowl to the floor before lifting it onto the trestletree which served as a rest.

As soon as the maids had put the water cowl in its place, the well digger arose and went over to have a look at the water. It was cloudier than usual, having just come from the well.

"Whew, what a mess!" he said and spat right into the water.

That was the most disgusting thing he could have done. Now the maids would have to pour out all the water and fetch another cowlful. To spit in the water, you know, children, is as wicked as tramping on bread.

The maids were furious at the man. One seized the cowl-staff and the other the big copper dipper, which hung on the side of the cowl, and went for him. "Clear out, you swine!" they shrieked at him. "What right have you here? You haven't got the manners of a decent hog."

The man was obliged to defend himself, and the uproar in the kitchen was deafening. In the midst of the fracas the door of the kitchen bedroom opened and Fru Lagerlöf appeared on the threshold.

"What on earth are you doing out here?" she asked.

They stopped at once. The stranger turned his back on the maids and greeted Mother respectfully.

"It is not so serious as it looks, Frua," he said.

"This beast spat in the water cowl," the maids shrieked, pointing to the man.

"I had to resort to a bit of ribaldry to awaken Frua," the well digger explained. "But I'll soon make up for it."

Then, grasping the water cowl by the handles, he carried it out of the kitchen and emptied the water he had polluted upon the stone step outside the door.

Mother, the housekeeper, and the two maids looked on in speechless amazement at the strength of the man. But they were to have greater proof of his strength later! Germund Germundsson now gripped the handle of the cowl with one hand and swung it onto his shoulder as easily as if it were a mug of ale, and, carrying it down to the well, began to refill it with water.

When Mother saw what the man was doing, she quickly sent a maid out with the cowlstaff, but he did not need it, he said. Grasping again the cowl by the handles, he carried it at arm's length across the stableyard into the kitchen and set it down on the trestletree.

By this feat he had redeemed himself in the eyes of everyone, and it was clear that he would be allowed to dig as many wells as he wished at Mårbacka. One does not say no to a man who can lift the roof off your house if he were so minded. As soon as Mother assured him that he might dig the well, he asked her where she would like to have it.

"It must lie in a spot where there is water in the ground," she said, "and as close as possible to the wash house, for it is there the water is most needed."

"If Frua wishes to have the well at the side of the wash house, that's where it's going to be," said Germund.

The following day he began digging just outside the wash house. No one had seen him go about with a divining rod or any other testing device. He seemed to be lord of all the water veins in the depths of the earth and could make them flow in whatever direction he saw fit.

He would have no help with the digging, but called for a couple of boys with wheelbarrows to remove the dirt and gravel he tossed up. He was a fast worker. Never in their lives had the boys been so driven! They had hardly got one barrow emptied before another was filled. Germund had staked off a space of about fifty square feet, and to dig that out was no slight task. But before evening, he had dug down so far that not even his head was visible.

Mother used to say that while Germund was digging the well she couldn't sit quietly sewing, for she wanted to see whether he could find water. Besides, it was fun to watch him at his work. She wouldn't have believed that a person could be so strong or have such tenacity of purpose.

Germund was pleased with the ground where he dug. He

declared that all the signs indicated that he would soon strike water. He had found no stones or hardpan, but when he had cleared away the top layer, he came upon dry sand, and by the time he had dug through that he would find water—of that he was certain.

But the gravel bed was deep, and Germund had to dig the next day also. The work did not go so fast now as on the previous day. He had to send for workmen to put up a shaft on which two men could stand to remove all the gravel he tossed up, and dump it at the side of the opening. But this device soon became inadequate. The excavation was now so deep that the men were obliged to rig up a pulley on which two barrels attached to long ropes could be moved up and down, as ore is drawn from the mines.

Toward evening of the third day, Mother became uneasy. Germund was digging deeper and deeper into the earth; still, no water came. If Mother had known the work was to last so long, she would never have undertaken it on her own initiative. She had hoped to surprise Father with this water, and now perhaps she had let herself in for something that could not be carried out successfully.

One day it rained, and water came pouring into the well from every direction. But it did not come from any well spring. It was surface water, which had to be bailed out; so it was some time before the well was dry.

Germund worked on and on. The men had to fetch a long ladder and lower it into the hole so that he could go up and down. But the ladder soon became too short, and they had to lengthen it with two additional ladders.

The worst of it was, they were in the midst of the harvest season. The hay was dry and should be taken in, and the rye was ripe and must be garnered. How to get the harvesting done, Mother did not know, for the farmhands were busy at the well from morning to night. All the other work was at a standstill.

Mother suggested to Germund that he stop digging, but he would not listen. Then she asked him if it would be advisable to try digging in some other place, but this he positively refused to do. Mother was at her wit's end. She had the feeling that he was capable of doing no end of harm if he were not allowed to finish the work he had set his heart upon.

Mother noticed one day that the rye was turning brown, which is a sign that it was so ripe that the kernels were ready to drop out of their beards. It would not do to put off the cutting any longer. Father was up at the Kymsberg Ironworks, of which he was the manager. So he was not far away, and Mother could have sent for him easily, but she did not wish to unless it became absolutely necessary. It would have hurt her pride, I think, to be obliged to admit that she could not manage the farm herself.

But just when the need was greatest, she had an inspiration. She went out to the well and begged Germund to come up from the hole, as she wished to speak to him. When he came up, he was covered from head to foot with mud and sand; so she could scarcely tell what he was made of.

Mother told him the rye must be cut next day and asked him to help with the work. The man threw up his big chin and grinned at her scornfully.

"Oh, I have cut rye in my day," he said with a lofty air, "but it is not the kind of work that is suitable for me."

"Nevertheless, rye is what we must all live upon," said Mother. "However much water we may get from your well, Germund, it will be of little use if we have no bread."

The well digger gave her a sharp glance from his dark eyes, but smiled rather indulgently, as if he were amused at a mere woman's daring to tell him the truth.

"Very well, Frua, it shall be as you wish. But I must have the longest scythe you've got on the farm, and plenty of hands to bind the rye."

That, Mother assured him, he should have. In the evening Germund inspected all the scythes on the farm, but found none that suited him. He actually withdrew his offer to help with the cutting. To expect a grown man to use such scythes! They were only toys for children to play with. So in the middle of the night, Mother had to send for a smith to forge a scythe two yards long.

Mother was up next morning at four o'clock when the farm laborers went to their work; for she feared Germund might offer some new objection. It was well she was on hand; otherwise, he probably would have crawled out of his bargain.

Germund, carrying the scythe over his shoulder, came with the other harvesters. He walked at the head of the laborers and was the first to start working. But when he had swung the scythe two or three times, he turned and looked back at the binders. And again he threatened to quit.

"What does this mean?" he demanded. "Am I to have only two binders? In that case, I may as well go home and lay me down to rest."

"These are two of the best binders we have on the farm," Mother informed him. But the well digger's only answer was a shrug.

"Oh," said Mother, "if it's nothing else that's wanting, I'll get you a binder who can work as fast as two men can cut. With the two you have now, perhaps that will be enough for you."

"Well, perhaps they'll do, if they're the right sort."

Mother hurried back to the house and went straight to the kitchen. "I want you to go out and bind sheaves for that presumptuous fellow," she said to the housekeeper, "and show him what you can do. It may teach him to have a little respect for the Mårbacka folk."

So Maja Persdotter, who could bind sheaves for two cutters, went out to the rye fields at once. Germund was able to give her and the two other binders all the work they could do.

So much rye had never been harvested at Mårbacka in a single day. When the other farmhands saw how rapidly Germund swung his scythe, they paused in their work and stared at him. Then, grasping their scythes, they went at the rye with a will, the blades falling before them like a shower of rain. And that was how the whole field was reaped in a single day.

It was a great relief to Mother to have the rye harvested, and so she thought Germund might as well be allowed to go back to his digging for a few days more. She soon found, however, that while Germund was at Mårbacka she would have no end of trouble and worry.

On the very day the rye was being reaped, a strange young girl came to the house. She walked up the steps, entered the hall, and went straight to the kitchen. Since the housekeeper and the maids were out binding sheaves, Mother was alone in the house. As the door opened, she looked up and wondered who the girl might be.

She was dressed like a gentlewoman, but her clothes were threadbare and so ill fitting it was apparent they had not been made for her. She was about twenty years old, of slight build, and painfully thin, but her hands were large and rough like those of a laborer. She could not be called pretty, nor was she ugly, for her face was round and her complexion clear and rosy. When Mother wished to describe her she would always say: "She was one of those nondescript women you do not remember until you have seen her a number of times."

"I should like to speak to Fru Lagerlöf," said the girl.

"You are speaking to her," Mother replied.

The young girl came nearer. "I am Johanna Octopius, daughter of Dean Octopius of Brunskog," she said and held out her hand.

While Mother was shaking hands with her, she tried to recall what she had heard about Dean Octopius and his family. Mother herself was a clergyman's daughter and related to all the clerical families in Värmland; so surely, she thought, she must know who the Octopius's were.

"But is not Dean Octopius dead?" she queried.

"He is, alas!" sighed the girl. "I lost both father and mother many years ago."

It was all clear to Mother now. Dean Octopius and his wife died within a short time of each other and were survived by an only child, a little girl who was not quite like other children. As no relatives had been found who could take the child, the poor thing had to remain with her father's successor in the capacity of a Cinderella. In return for her services she was given food, shelter, and such clothing as had been discarded. She was by no means a fool, yet it could not be said that she was blessed with sound common sense. Mother guessed at once that this was the same Johanna Octopius who had now come to Mårbacka. But what in the world was she doing here?

Johanna Octopius, however, was not long in stating her errand. She had come to ask Mother if she might stay here for a few days.

"It is not unlikely that you may," Mother told her, "but first I should like to know why you wish to stop here."

The poor girl flushed perceptibly. Evidently she had not expected to be questioned. She stood nervously pulling at a finger, not knowing what to answer, for she was painfully shy. When at last she spoke, it was with an air of mystery and in a voice so low as to be almost inaudible:

"I was ordered to come here."

"Is there anyone here whom you wish to see?"

The girl looked even more distressed. "I have never been able to lie," she said. "So I won't tell you if there's anyone here I want to see. I came to this house in answer to a command I received yesterday—to be on hand when I was needed."

Mother knew from her answer that the girl was not right in her head. She thought, however, it was best to let her stay at Mårbacka until there was an opportunity to send her home. Mother said, "Go into the room off the kitchen and rest yourself while I prepare the supper. You see, I have no servants in the house today; they are all out in the field binding sheaves."

Johanna Octopius said she was not tired and offered to help Mother get the supper. Mother soon found that, though the girl was willing, she was awkward and bungled everything she touched. She carried in wood and made up a fire, but she put so much salt in the porridge that no one could have eaten it; so it had to be thrown away, and the fresh pot of porridge she let burn.

At eight o'clock, the men came into the kitchen to eat.

Johanna Octopius stood at the stove dishing out the scorched porridge. When the well digger saw her he ripped out an oath, and Johanna Octopius dropped a big ladleful of the porridge on the fire. The smell of the burning porridge in the kitchen became insufferable. None of the men, however, exchanged a look or a word.

The following day, the housekeeper informed Mother that the well digger had told Lill-Bengt that that crazy daughter of a clergyman had fallen in love with him the spring he dug a well at Brunskog Rectory. At first he was flattered, he had said, because a girl of the upper class had taken a fancy to him, but after awhile he hated the very sight of her. She pursued him wherever he went, and he'd never get rid of the girl unless he killed her.

Mother had suspected from the first that a love affair lay behind the mysterious call. Now that the mystery was solved, Mother ordered Lill-Bengt to get ready at once and drive Mamselle Octopius back to Brunskog. Then she talked to the girl and tried to make her realize how unseemly her behavior was. Did she not see that she was lowering herself by running after a man who did not want her? And, finally, she told the girl that she must go home, and that it would not be worth her while to come back.

Johanna Octopius bent before the storm of reproof like the frail reed that she was. Without a protest she seated herself in the cart and drove away from Mårbacka.

When Lill-Bengt had driven about two miles, one of the pegs that fastened the traces to the harness came loose, and he had to get down to tighten it. He was only a moment, but in the meantime, Johanna Octopius seized the opportunity to make her escape. Before the driver discovered her flight, she had disappeared in the woods nearby. He tried to catch her, but on account of the horse, he could not go very far. And so she eluded him.

To steal away and disappear, to run like water one tries to hold between the hands, was the only thing the girl could do to perfection, and must have practiced at that all her life.

Lill-Bengt had to turn around and drive back to

Mårbacka. As Johanna Octopius did not appear again that day, Mother wondered if the poor girl had done herself some harm. She was sorry now that she had spoken harshly to her.

The next morning the runaway came into the cow barn and asked for a glass of milk. While she was drinking it, the dairymaid quietly sent for the mistress, but when Mother came out to speak to Johanna, she had already gone.

The well digger was in a rage. One side of the shaft had collapsed, filling the opening with sand. Whenever that crazy Hanna appeared, things always went wrong with him, he said. He never in his life had laid violent hands upon anyone, but if that woman continued to pursue him, he would have to rid himself of her some way or other.

Mother was sure that something dreadful would happen. She had had that feeling from the first day Germund came to the house. She wrote to the dean of Brunskog, begging him to send for the girl, but to no avail. Then she tried to capture her in order to shut her up. But the girl was on her guard and took to her heels the moment anyone approached.

One day Johanna Octopius came stealing across the yard and up to the well hole; she stopped and peered down into the deep excavation. Germund, who was down at the bottom of the well, must have felt her presence, for in a moment he appeared at the top of the ladder, shrieking and cursing. Although she fled instantly, he hurled stones and gravel after her as if she had been a mangy cur. Johanna Octopius, however, was not to be frightened away; she stole about the grounds as before.

And then one morning, when there had been about all the mishaps that could possibly occur during the digging of a well, when the hole was so deep that one who stood at the bottom could see the stars moving across the sky, though on the surface it was broad day, a man came dancing into the kitchen shouting: "Water! Water!"

Mother, the housekeeper, and the maids ran out. They bent over the well, peering into its depths, and, sure enough, far down at the bottom of the hole they beheld a shining mirror of water.

There is something almost miraculous about finding water in that way on a farm. Mother had had a trying time and had often wished she had never ordered the digging. But now that water had come, she thanked God from her heart for this great blessing. Then she asked after Germund.

"He is still down there," answered one of the men. "Maybe he wants to see whether it's a real water vein he has struck."

They called down to him, but he did not answer. One of the men was about to descend to see whether anything had happened to him, when Germund placed his foot on the lowest rung of the ladder.

He mounted slowly, feeling for the rungs with one hand and holding the other to his eyes. They thought he had got sand in his eyes.

When he reached the top rung, he put out his hand gropingly. Two men sprang to his aid. It was almost impossible to get him on solid ground again. He had only to put out his foot and take a step, the men told him, but he was afraid.

"My dear Germund, we are so glad you have found water," said Mother.

"Ah, Frua, that water was dearly bought! Just as the water gushed forth down there, something that felt like smoke flew into my eyes. And now I can't see."

When they finally had him on firm ground, he threw himself down on the grass and pressed both hands against his eyes. The men stood silent, waiting for him to rise. None of them liked him, but they thought it dreadful if he should lose his sight.

In a moment he rose to a sitting posture. "There's still the same darkness," he said. "It is all over with me, for I am blind."

Mother tried to reassure him. "It will soon pass," she said. "You were down there in the dark too long, and you have not yet become accustomed to the daylight."

"No, it isn't that," he said. "My eyes burn as though they were on fire. Oh, what is to become of me!"

With that he leaped to his feet, raised his arm high, and

tried to jump into the well. The men rushed forward and barred his way, but he flung them all aside.

"Let me be!" he roared. "I want to die down there!"

It was horrible! The men tried to restrain him, and in the struggle, he lost his sense of direction and ran round and round in circles, shrieking and cursing and clutching at the air as if trying to capture someone.

"Show me where the well lies," he shouted, "or I'll crush the life out of the first man I lay my hands on."

He raved like a madman, but luckily no tragedy occurred, for the people ran out of his way, and he himself, fortunately, got nowhere near the well. Again he threw himself down on the grass. Every part of his body twitched and jerked convulsively, and, clenching his fists, he broke out again and again into wild threats.

While he lay there in a rage so menacing that no man would have dared go near him, the half-witted girl, Johanna Octopius, approached. She came in her usual quiet way, so that no one was aware of her presence until she was close beside him.

Mother was about to rush forward and warn her, but she had already laid her hand on his.

"Don't curse so, Germund," she said in her low, soft voice. "I am here to help you."

Everyone thought that he would seize her by the throat and choke her to death. He suddenly burst into a horrible, savage laugh, but he did not harm her.

"I am here," she said again. "*They* knew this would happen, and *They* sent me here. I was born into this world for no other purpose than to help you."

There must have been something about her that did him good, for he took her hands and laid them against his burning eyes.

"Thou mad Hanna!" he said. "Oh, thou mad Hanna!"

"What does it matter that you are blind?" she said. "I will be eyes to you."

In his misery and utter helplessness, it was a comfort to know there was someone who cared for him, whether he was blind or seeing, weak or strong, good or bad, rich or poor.

Mother, meanwhile, remained close by. She was not quite sure how this would end, when she heard Germund say:

"It is soothing to have your hand on my eyes."

Then Mother felt easy in her mind and beckoned the others to come away and leave them alone. You see, she knew that a great miracle had taken place. Love had found the way. It was God's will from the beginning that those two should be together.

When we have thanked Aunt Nana for telling us the story of the well, we say that the good water really deserved to have a story of its own.

"You have a wonderful memory, Nana," Aunt Lovisa remarks, "to be able to recall so many of Mother's old stories! I recollect, of course, her telling us that the man who dug the well went blind, but his name and all the details I had quite forgotten."

Papa also says that Aunt Nana is wonderful. "But are you quite certain that the girls' name was Octopius? It sounds so unfamiliar."

Aunt Nana laughs. "You are right, that was not the girl's real name; as I did not wish to give her right name, I invented a fictitious one."

"As every true narrator should, to be sure," Papa observes.

"But, Nana, what made you think of that particular story tonight?" Mamma queries.

"Well, you see"—Aunt Nana drawls a bit—"it is rather difficult to explain. Perhaps it was because I've heard so much talk about the pond the last few days...."

Elin Laurell now puts a query: "Do you really believe, Fru Hammargren, that love always leads us aright? Should not one first question it critically instead of accepting it blindly?"

Aunt Nana ponders a long moment before she answers:

"I believe that love invariably leads us aright, Fröken Laurell. But it takes great courage and faith to obey its

94

promptings, and that, alas, is what we all lack."

Papa usually keeps all the Värmland papers in a small cupboard at the back of his writing table. The next day he asks me to put away the paper Aunt Nana was reading before she got her bad headache. While I am folding the paper, I see on the front page two or three round blotches that look like dried-in tears. I verily believe the newspaper, the headache, and the story are somehow linked together, but in what way I do not know. And because I am so young, no one will tell me. So now I think I shall never know.

ELIN LAURELL

Aline Laurell has come back to pay us a visit; we have not seen her since she moved to West Ämtervik last autumn. Aline is her own sweet self again, though perhaps a trifle thinner, but she looks so well and happy. All the old unpleasantness seems to have been forgotten.

Papa, Mamma, Elin, Anna, Gerda, and I are all out on the porch to welcome her, and she hugs and kisses us all, except Papa, of course. Anna and Gerda seem to be as glad to see her as I am, and she kisses them just as affectionately as she kisses me. It is well that Aline does not know they think more of Elin than they do of her.

They say, those two, that Elin is such a pleasant teacher and so nice about the lessons; that she is not so strict as Aline, and doesn't give us such long lessons to learn; nor does she get angry if we cannot answer all her questions. But I don't care about shorter lessons! I like Aline the best, anyhow, and no one can make me care more for Elin.

But I must confess that it is difficult not to like Elin. To be sure, she is pleasing and tells us many interesting things. Sometimes she chats with us during school hours until there is little time left for our lessons. This pleases Anna and Gerda, of course. I also think her entertaining, but I don't believe her way is right. Certainly, Aline did not teach us in that way.

When Elin examines our papers, she sometimes passes over a mistake without marking it, but if I speak of this to Anna, she says it doesn't matter. "I learn much more from Elin than I learned from Aline," she declares; "for Elin knows more than is printed in books."

Anna, no doubt, is right about that, but just the same I don't want to like Elin, I would rather be faithful to Aline. It is a good thing that Elin is plain. Her nose is too short. It looks as if the tip had been cut off, and her complexion is

96

sallow, and she has a wart on one cheek. And besides, she has a double chin, like Field Marshal Klingspor in the story of *Ensign Stål*. But she has a beautiful head of fair hair which is always well-dressed, and I must say that she has a tall, graceful figure. Then, too, she has a beautiful voice, and there is something about her that's different.

Now when Mamma comes into a room, you know by her manner and bearing that she is from Filipstad, for there is something about her of its iron and its forges, and when Aline comes into a room she brings with her something of Karlstad, of its schools and its gay social life. But when Elin enters a room she brings the whole world with her. She is equally at home in Greece and in Egypt, in Greenland and in Australia. She knows what people are thinking wherever human beings are to be found. She knows so much about the ancients, too, and above all, she keeps in touch with everything modern.

But now that Aline has come, I'm glad I have been faithful to her and have never told Elin things I wouldn't tell anyone else. I have never told her about *Oceola* or my reading of the Bible so that Papa might get well.

Elin has been kind to me all the time. She tried at first to make me talk to her freely, as I talked to Aline, but she soon gave that up. And when I cried so terribly at having to go to the Sunne ball, Elin did not lift a finger to help me. When she and I happen to be alone in the nursery, we sit there, sometimes for hours, without exchanging a word. So Elin must have seen that I am trying to dislike her.

The second day Aline was here she looked at me strangely and asked why I was so silent—was I not feeling well? The third day, after dinner, she asked me if I would like to go for a walk. But she did not include any of the others. I was glad of a chance to be alone with Aline. "We'll have a pleasant hour together," I thought; "just we two," as Aline used to say, as though she and I were of the same age.

She was silent as we walked down the avenue, and when

we came to the road, she pulled off my mitten and drew my hand into her muff, between her two warm hands.

"My dear child," she said, "how cold you are!"

Aline always used to draw my hand into her muff when we went out together, for it has always been hard for me to keep warm. I am glad that she has taken my hand into her muff once more.

"Now you must tell me," she said, "how you are getting on with your writing."

"But, Aline, don't you remember that I told you I wouldn't write stories until I grew up?"

"There is something I must say to you," Aline began rather hesitantly. "Now don't be angry with me. I have thought that perhaps it was wrong for me to let you talk so much about your ambition to write."

"Why, Aline?"

"Well, you see, I may have been partly to blame for your indulging these fancies. But I thought it might be possible that you had inherited a little talent for writing. Your paternal aunt, Nana Hammargren, is a very clever *raconteuse*, and your maternal uncle, Kristofer, is a remarkably gifted man, as far as I am able to judge. And besides you are related to the poet Tegnér."

"Are we related to Tegnér?"

"Don't you know you are?" said Aline, astonished.

"It seems strange that your father has not told you. There is no one he admires so much as Tegnér, but I daresay he is too modest to let his own children know of the relationship. Your paternal grandfather's mother and Tegnér's mother were sisters; so your grandfather and Tegnér were first cousins. That is why I thought you would have a leaning toward authorship."

Aline paused as if she expected an answer; but I was speechless. I tried to withdraw my hand from the muff, but she held it firmly.

"You know," she continued, "it is the most dangerous thing that can happen to a person—to nourish an illusion that he is to become something out of the ordinary, if the

98

necessary powers are lacking. Later, when it becomes evident that he has not the requisite talent, he usually becomes a misanthrope and a lamentable failure. It is easy to uproot such fancies when one is still a child, but afterward it is almost impossible.

Aline was serious. It was hard for her to tell me what she felt she must say. I know that I have often talked freely with her about my desire to write stories, although at the time I did not take the matter very seriously. Therefore, I didn't much mind what Aline had just said, but I asked her how she had found out that I had not the ability to become a writer.

"When I went away from here last autumn," she said, "it was partly for your sake—that you might have a teacher with more knowledge and experience than I have. I thought Elin would be just the teacher you needed. But Elin says she does not think there is anything exceptional about you. At least, there is no indication of it yet; she does not think you more gifted than the other children. You will be angry with me, I fear, but it is much better that you should know this now, before it is too late. Anyhow, you can become a fine woman."

I feel a little hurt, but it is not worth mentioning. For I have never really believed I have any talent for writing, and now that Elin thinks I have no unusual ability, I take the matter calmly.

"You are not crying, dear, are you?" says Aline. She speaks gently but her voice sounds troubled.

"No, dear Aline, I'm not crying. You are very kind to tell me this."

Aline is silent for a moment, after which she tells me that she is betrothed. I am so amazed that I forget all she has said to me before. Then she informs me that she is to marry a childhood friend whose name is Adolf Arnell. He is the one she has loved all her life, she says. She thought, at times, he had ceased to care for her, but his seeming indifference was due to the fact that his circumstances made it impossible for him to marry. When she left Mårbacka, it had been nearly

99

over between them, but now all is well again and she is very happy.

I rejoice in her happiness and am glad that she has told me of this herself. I think she must have told Mamma and Elin, but no one else, except me. Aline probably knows that I am fonder of her than are either Anna or Gerda. And so when we come back from our stroll, Aline and I are as fast friends as before she went away.

After we remove our wraps, Aline steps into the bedroom to speak to Mamma, but I go straight to the kitchen bedroom, where Elin Laurell is sitting, as usual, discoursing on predestination with Aunt Lovisa.

"You think, then, Elin, that it's all a matter of chance?" Auntie says.

"No," says Elin, "I don't believe it's merely a matter of chance. I think that if a person really makes up his mind to do a thing he can do it."

Although I had not been discouraged by what Aline had told me, I feel thankful to Elin for what she has said. Perhaps I can become a writer if it depends only on the will and not on talent. For will—I think I have.

I feel attracted to Elin the moment she says that about the will. Drawing close to her side, I listen eagerly to everything she says. Without thinking, I lay a hand upon her shoulder. She turns her head toward me and smiles. And then I remember that I want to be loyal to Aline and not to like Elin; at least, I mean not to let her see that I do. Suddenly it occurs to me that Aline no longer cares whether or not a little girl at Mårbacka likes her. Aline has a sweetheart now and is going to be married. So I am quite free to like Elin as much as I wish. And now I am just as good friends with Elin as ever I was with Aline, and even better perhaps.

THE STOCKHOLM DIARY

*God comfort me, poor child, who cannot
go back to that faded wallpaper and
those rag mattings for at least half a
year...*

The doubts Aline Laurell has raised in Selma about
her talent for writing are compounded by doubts about
the attractiveness of her character, as Nurse Maja
warns her not to "sit and mope" while she is a guest at
the elegant home of her Uncle Oriel and Aunt Georgina
in Stockholm. Fears that she may be either too dull or
too wild for her city relatives occupy her thoughts. With
courage and pluck she gets on, buoyed by a romantic
fantasy about the young student she meets on the train,
and by the very act of keeping a journal to record and
reflect on her experience. Though Selma surely did
keep a day-book of this kind during the visit, these
excerpts are from a work composed many years later
from her notes, memories, and imagination. *The Diary
of Selma Lagerlöf* was the third in Lagerlöf's published
memoirs, and is devoted entirely to the Stockholm trip.
— G. A.

THE JOURNEY TO STOCKHOLM

Monday, January 20, 1873

On the train from Kil to Laxå.

Elin Laurell gave me a lovely daybook for Christmas. It has a dainty white binding, a blue back and gilt edges. It is such a pretty book it seems almost a pity to write in it.

"But that is just what it's for," Elin said, and that I should accustom myself to jotting down all that happens to me from day to day, as it will be useful to me and a pleasure in after-years.

I hardly think that I should have kept a diary had I stayed at home, as nothing ever happens in winter at Mårbacka. One day is exactly like another. But now that I'm going to Stockholm, I have put the book in my bag and am taking it with me.

The train shakes dreadfully, and my hands are numb with the cold, but I don't mind much. The worst of it is I do not know how one usually writes in a daybook.

A short time ago I read *The Daughters of the President,* by Fredrika Bremer, which is almost like a diary from beginning to end. But I do not care to write in that wise and learned way. Nor do I think it is a real daybook—I mean the kind that folks keep to themselves and let no one read except an intimate friend. Now if Fredrika Bremer were seated in a corner of this compartment with pencil and book in hand, what would she record? Well, first she would probably tell what took place this morning as Daniel and I were leaving home. But that would make a sorry beginning.

Elin Laurell says that if one is to become an author one must be thankful for every experience and glad, too, if one meets with trials that are hard to bear, for otherwise, one cannot describe how it feels to be unhappy.

So perhaps I had better jot down what Nurse Maja told

103

me before I left for Stockholm. It may be of use to me when I'm old enough to write novels.

Still, it was a pity, for until then I had been so happy in the thought of the journey. I had fared so well at the home of my uncle five years ago, and the exercises at the Institute had made me well and strong. Anyhow, I am glad to have the company of Daniel on the journey. He is going back to Upsala after the Christmas holidays. Daniel is always kind and considerate, and I think the world of him!

Having to get up at three this morning was not pleasant, but we had to do it in order to arrive at Kil station in time to catch the train for Stockholm. Everyone, except Papa, of course, was up to bid Daniel and me good-bye. I thought they all looked forlorn as they sat round the coffee table, but that was perhaps because they were sleepy and half frozen. I was sleepy and cold, too, but I was happy, and laughed and chattered. Aunt Lovisa remarked that evidently I was not sorry to be leaving home. She seemed to think it was wrong of me to be glad.

"Don't you think, Auntie, it would be a shame for me to be sad when Papa and Mamma are giving me this costly trip that I may have treatment for my leg?" But Aunt Lovisa would never listen to reason. Her only reply was that she was the sort who could never leave home without regret, though, of course, it was only foolish of her.

Mother, obviously wishing to end the discussion between Auntie and me, arose, saying that it was time we were off. But before we left, I wanted to go out to the kitchen to say good-bye to the housekeeper and the maids; for I was to be away until spring.

As I passed through the bedroom on my way to the kitchen, Nurse Maja stopped me and asked if she might have a word with me. She looked so mysterious and solemn that I became quite alarmed. I stopped, of course, to hear what she had to tell me.

It seems that last summer she overheard Fru Wallroth ask Fru Afzelius whether it was true that Selma was to come to them next winter and take treatments at the Institute.

"Yes," Fru Afzelius had answered, "it is true." And then she had added that it was not surprising her parents wished to send Selma to Stockholm, but both she and her husband would rather have had one of the other girls, for Selma was so dull and unresponsive.

When Nurse Maja told me that, my heart was crushed. I stood stock-still, not knowing what to answer.

"You mustn't be angry with me, Selma, for telling you this," Nurse Maja said. "I mean it for your good. I only wanted to warn you so you wouldn't sit and mope, as you do sometimes, but be chatty and gay when you get to Stockholm. I think you are the nicest of all the Mårbacka children, and I want everyone else to think so, too. That was why I had to tell you."

While she was talking I tried to think of a crushing retort—At last I hit upon something telling and to the point!

"Don't you remember that it says in the catechism, *'If you hear any evil of another, do not repeat it; for silence hurts no one. You shall tell it neither to friend nor to foe; and reveal it not if you can consciously avoid it.'*"

With that, I walked away, feeling that I had given Nurse Maja the rebuke she deserved for her talebearing. My distress was less acute now, but I was not nearly so sure of myself as I had been a moment earlier. When I said good-bye to Aunt Lovisa I kissed her hand. I think she understood that I wished to beg her pardon for admonishing her.

And when Mother wrapped her big fur coat around me to keep me nice and warm on the long drive to the train station at Kil, I nearly burst out crying. I felt so sorry to be leaving her and all those who loved me, to go to others who would rather not have me!

When I got up into the sleigh my heart ached dreadfully. I feared it would ache like that all the while I was in Stockholm. How should I be able to endure it until spring!

Daniel is studying medicine at Upsala; so perhaps he could help me. When I asked him what one did for anyone who suffered pain in the heart, he only laughed and said that he would answer my question some other time; he was too sleepy now.

We said nothing more to one another during the drive to Kil. Even if I couldn't be a jolly traveling companion, at least I would not be fussy and troublesome.

At Kil we bought third-class tickets, and when the train arrived we were ushered into an empty compartment in which the odors of gin, foot sweat and I know not what else assailed our nostrils. We tried to air the place, but it grew so cold that we had to close the window again. I told Daniel that when I was rich I'd never travel third class.

Daniel gave me a look that took me in from head to foot and said in a casual tone, "Then I think you will have to travel third class as long as you live."

I couldn't help thinking of the passage in the Bible where it says, "*Mene, mene, tekel, upharsin,*" for today I have been measured and weighed and counted—and found wanting.

When the train began to move, Daniel took out a German anatomy and settled himself in a corner to study, while I took out my diary and began to write.

And now I have written five whole pages. It really is quite necessary to keep a diary. Looking up, I see that we have come all the way to Laxå station. The time has passed quickly despite the pain in my heart and my sadness— thanks to Elin Laurell!

On the train from Laxå to Katrineholm.

Here we are seated again, Daniel with his anatomy, I with my diary. Now I must record what took place at Laxå. It is remarkable how the time flies when one is writing!

At Laxå, Daniel closed his book and said, "Here we eat dinner." We had brought a large hamper from home, and I asked him to help me take it down from the rack. He would-n't hear of it, however, and said it was no pleasure to eat on the train; we'd go over to the station restaurant instead and get a hot meal. Indeed I had no objection, and as we hurried across the tracks, Daniel told me to eat quickly, as we had only twenty minutes until our train would leave.

106

In the middle of the dining room there was a large table with all kinds of tempting dishes—almost more than at a Christmas party, and against the wall, round about it, were side tables and chairs where one could sit down to eat. Daniel went over to one of the side tables and, pointing to a chair, said:

"You'd better sit here, Selma. I'll bring you your dinner."

As I am fourteen years old, I thought I might at least be allowed to select the food for myself. There was a great variety of savory dishes set out on the big table, and Daniel brought me nothing that I would have liked. But I dared not move from the chair where he had told me to sit, for fear I might do something awkward. Many travelers were crowding around the center table—what if one of them should give me a push and I should spill a whole bowl of gravy over myself? Then Daniel would be sure to think that I ought to travel *fourth* class all my life. I had had only two dishes, but I told Daniel that that was enough and that I wanted no dessert. Indeed I was far from satisfied, but I was afraid we would miss the train if I ordered dessert. Daniel himself ate his dessert with perfect ease, and then he stepped into the adjoining room, where there was a large coffee table, and poured out a cup for himself.

The travelers began to troop out of the dining room, and I became uneasy lest the train should start and we be left behind.

But Daniel seemed to be in no haste. When he went over to the desk to pay the bill, he walked so slowly that I should have liked to run up and push him along.

When at last he had paid, I thought that we surely would go to take our seats in the train. But then Daniel met a fellow student with whom he stopped to chat. It looked as though he had entirely forgotten that we were to leave by this train. I was as certain as anything that we would be too late, but I dared not remind Daniel, for then he would have been eager to show me how sure he was of himself and how accustomed he was to traveling. Then we would have had to stay in Laxå until the following day. At all events, he stood

107

there talking until the stationmaster came to the door and called out the Stockholm train. Then, at last, he beckoned to me, and we went out of the dining room.

We had just taken our seats in the compartment when I missed my muff. I told Daniel that I must have left it in the restaurant. He dashed out of the train and over to the dining room, leaving me all alone in the compartment. I am very fond of my muff, for Mother ordered it made for me from the skin of one of our turkeys. It is pure white with a rose-colored lining. But now I was sorry that I had told Daniel of my loss. Supposing the train should leave before he found the muff! I heard the conductor go through the train closing the doors, and I was afraid he would shut our door before Daniel got back. But just as the conductor had reached the door of our compartment, Daniel came running alongside the train and managed to climb aboard. He had the muff in his hand, but he was so furious because of my carelessness that he flung the muff at me and said there was no need of my forgetting it, as I had nothing else to think about.

As to that, he was quite right.

Now Daniel has dropped off to sleep over his anatomy, but I am not asleep. I'm thinking what a pity it is that I am not only dull and unresponsive but absent-minded and stupid as well!

I can't write any more, for when we reached Katrineholm station the student whom Daniel had met at Laxå came into our compartment in order to have someone to chat with, and it is impossible to write while they sit beside me talking.

Between Södertälje and Stockholm.

Now I'll have to hurry, for I want to write a few lines to say that I am no longer sad, and my heart has stopped aching, and that is a blessed relief.

I know that we're nearing Stockholm, but I could not write before because the student sat with us until we came to Södertälje, when he said he must go back to his compartment to gather up his things before we arrived.

There were many old women down by the station who offered small cakes for sale in little bags. I got two bags, one from the student and one from Daniel. It was very nice of them, although I have to admit those cakes were pretty stale.

But now I must hasten to write about what took place after the student came into our compartment. First, he talked with Daniel, of course; then after a little, Daniel told him that I was his sister and my name was Selma and that I was going to Stockholm to stay until spring.

"How delightful for Selma!" said the student. Then he told us that his parents were Stockholmers, but they resided now in Christiania. They loved Sweden more than any other country and wished their son to be brought up a Swede, and so he had grown up in the home of relatives in Stockholm. To his mind Stockholm was the best place in the whole world. The last two winters he had been at the University of Upsala and had spent the Christmas holidays in Christiania. But for life and gaiety, it couldn't be compared to Stockholm.

"But you'll see for yourself, Selma, how it is, " he said.

I answered, of course, that five years ago I had lived in Stockholm a whole winter and knew the city well.

"Five years ago!" said the astonished student. "But you were only a child then, so you couldn't have seen very much of it."

"I did though," I replied. "I saw the whole city."

The student really must have loved Stockholm, for he asked me whether I had seen this or that or that, and there was not much that I was not familiar with. He said I must have a good memory, and thought it remarkable that I had seen so many interesting things although I was but nine years old at the time.

The student and I became the best of friends, and before long he spoke only to me. For Daniel had merely passed through Stockholm on his way to Upsala; so he did not know the city as well as I did.

If Anna or Hilda Wallroth or Emma Laurell had been sitting here, opposite the student, they would surely have fallen in love with him, for he is so good-looking!

109

He has dark hair that curls over his forehead and one unruly lock that keeps falling down when he grows enthusiastic. He has large eyes that are so dark that I can't tell what color they are, but they scintillate like black jewels. And he is also friendly and sympathetic. I wonder if he saw that I was sad when he came in, and if that was why he spoke to me?

Naturally Daniel thought that what I said was not worth listening to, so he took up his book and began to read again. But I noticed that he was not very intent upon his reading, for all of a sudden he chuckled at something that was said.

Nurse Maja flashed across my mind as we were at the most interesting part of our conversation. It would have been well if she had sat in a corner of the compartment and heard how easily I talked with the student.

I thought, too, that when I came to Stockholm, it would be a slight matter for me to show Aunt and Uncle that I was neither dull nor unresponsive. All I would have to do would be to sit down and talk to them as easily and frankly as I now talked with the student. Indeed, he did not find me dull; nor did Daniel, who sat chuckling behind his book.

The student and I discussed many topics besides Stockholm before we reached Södertälje. It was so easy to talk with him; we were of one mind on many subjects, and I was not afraid to say quite freely what I thought.

When he went his way at Södertälje, the compartment became singularly empty. But I was not at all depressed as I had been earlier in the day. I felt a bit giddy, as I feel even at this moment. Daniel says, "Now we are in Stockholm!" Auntie and Uncle are on the platform awaiting us.

Late evening in the nursery at Uncle Oriel's.

It was kind of Uncle Oriel and Aunt Georgina to come down to the station to meet us. I know that the station in Stockholm does not lie far away, as it did five years ago, but is only a stone's throw from Klara Strandgata, where they live. All the same it was kind of them.

They seemed to be happy to see us and asked whether we had had a pleasant journey, and if we were tired, and how the folks were at Mårbacka. They certainly didn't show it if they were sorry to receive me.

But I must say that although I had been so sure of myself on the train but a short time before, I couldn't help thinking the moment I saw them of what Nurse Maja had told me. No, it did not turn out as Nurse Maja believed, that her tittle-tattle would make me more talkative and gay. On the contrary, I was struck dumb.

Luckily Daniel was with me and did the talking. He conveyed greetings from home and said that he had had a wonderful rest during the many holidays, and that there had been good sleighing every day and jolly Christmas parties both at Gårdsjö and Eriksberg and at Mårbacka.

I marveled at Daniel, who was always at his ease with people, and that was why everybody liked him.

We had only a few steps to go before we came to Uncle's gate, which was well, for we had been up since three o'clock in the morning. As soon as the gate opened, Fru Blomkvist, the porteress, jerked the little red curtain back from the wicket and gave us a stern and searching glance. It looked as if she took us for thieves who were trying to sneak in to steal the landlord's (Duke d'Otrante's) silver. I knew Fru Blomkvist and her curtain and her stern looks very well since last I lived in this house, and thought it really amusing that she was the same old sixpence.

When we had mounted a flight of stairs and stood in the hall of the apartment, I recognized the hangers and the hat racks and the shelf of galoshes which I had used five years ago. I was allowed to put my things in the same places where they had been before. I felt, as it were, more at home now and not so terribly strange.

As we came into the apartment proper, I knew the place at once, but it looked finer and more spacious than it was as I remembered it. Directly opposite the entrance hall is the dining room, adjoining it is the parlor, and beyond that lies the bedroom and back of it the nursery. On the other side of

111

the dining room is Uncle's room, and back of that, again, the kitchen, the maids' room, their dining room, and their wardrobe. Auntie and Uncle really have a large and beautiful apartment; it would be a shame not to be contented here. In the parlor, the bedroom and Uncle's room, the floors are covered with rugs and the walls covered with fine paintings. All the wallpaper is whole and unfaded; the curtains are stiff, and hang straight as if they had been put up only a day or two ago; the ceilings are ornamented with pretty figures in plaster, and there is a polished mahogany bookcase filled with row upon row of choice volumes. In the parlor stands a large whatnot filled with dainty porcelain figurines. Yes, it is elegant here.

But I couldn't help thinking of a place where the only pictures on the walls are of fishermen angling by torchlight and a pietist spoiling the merriment at a supper dance, which we got as a Christmas premium from the *Family Journal*—now *Past and Present*. At home we have porcelain figurines, but they are kept in a plain corner cupboard. There the wallpaper is faded, and on the floors are only rag carpets.

But God comfort me, poor child, who cannot go back to that faded wallpaper and those rag mattings for at least half a year!

After tea, Auntie said that Daniel and I had better go to bed at once, as we had been traveling all day. Daniel was to sleep in Uncle's room, and I was to sleep on the sofa in the nursery with Cousin Elin and old Ulla Myhrman, who had been Uncle's housekeeper in his bachelor days.

But tired as I was I couldn't sleep, but lay tossing and turning. When I heard that the others were asleep, I lighted the candle and set down in the diary this last, hoping it would turn my thoughts away from all I had experienced that day by putting it all down. Besides, it is fun to keep a diary—almost more fun than reading novels.

But I hear the watchman in the Klara Tower toot twelve; so I shall have to leave off now and put out the light.

THE FIRST WEEK

January 21, 1873

Written by Ulla's small lamp.

I wonder if those who keep a diary ever record their dreams? For I would like to write about a strange dream I had last night that I cannot put out of my mind.

In the first place, I don't understand why I should have dreamed about Marit of Sotbråten. I remember, of course, that when Gerda was a small child, Nurse Maja used to tell her about a poor girl who was called Marit of Sotbråten. She lived at Högbergssäter, where Maja came from, and she was as mean and foolish as Maja was wise and kind. She always ran about unwashed and snotty, her tangled hair hanging over her eyes. One couldn't imagine a girl like Marit of Sotbråten ever combing her hair, and as for her clothes— they were nothing but rags. She seemed more akin to the trolls of Storsnipan than to human beings, Nurse Maja declared, and she was never known to do anything but raise mischief.

And if some morning Gerda wouldn't be washed or have her hair combed, then Marit of Sotbråten, seated on the highest peak of Storsnipan, laughed and shrieked for joy, as her greatest delight was to see unwashed and uncombed children of the gentry. And if Gerda would not go to sleep of an evening, but wanted to hear more stories, then Marit of Sotbråten came riding across the hills to crawl into bed with her. As she rode down the Käglabacken, the stones rolling before and behind, striking sparks and rumbling like a thunderstorm, there was nothing for Gerda to do but to draw the covers over her ears and go to sleep in a jiffy, to escape the horrid bedfellow.

Nurse Maja, however, never attempted to frighten me with Marit of Sotbråten, for I was too old and wise to believe such ridiculous tales. For that reason it seems strange that

113

Marit should have followed me here to Stockholm.

Just the same, I dreamed last night that I lay on the pretty white sofa in the nursery, when I saw sitting above me on the arm of the sofa, a filthy, repulsive girl. She sat swinging her legs and tossed her head so that the tufts of matted hair flew in every direction. I knew at once that she was Marit of Sotbråten. I was both frightened and angry and ordered her to go back to Högbergssäter at once. Then she crept in under the bedcovers, where she quickly became as small and narrow as an earthworm. Before I knew what she meant to do she had crawled into my ear. It was such a horrible sensation—having a long worm crawling around in my head—that I gave a shriek and with that, I awoke.

I know now that I had only been dreaming and that Marit of Sotbråten has not followed me to Stockholm. And yet, I could not shake off the sensation that a worm was crawling around in my head. And while I lay there half awake and tormented by my fear of the worm, I felt almost certain that Nurse Maja had sent Marit upon me because I had rebuked her for talebearing, quoting Scripture as my authority.

Nurse Maja was born at Högbergssäter, where there are a lot of witches who can send sickness and other ills upon those they have an evil eye for. Of course, I wouldn't say positively that the witches had taught their tricks to Maja, but I was not so far from believing they had. She was angry with me for ignoring her good intentions, and wanted to be avenged. And now I was no longer Selma Lagerlöf, but had turned into a wicked and foolish little imp whose name was Marit of Sotbråten.

It all seemed so real and true that I was frightened to the point of despair, and I cried a long while over my plight before I fell asleep again. Next morning, I was my old self, and then I laughed at myself for having imagined anything so absurd. But I wondered if, after all, there was not some truth in that dream.

I know it is only imagination, but why should I be so

irritable and so mistrustful of everyone and everything? I must have become a regular Marit of Sotbråten!

This morning Aunt Georgina told me that she had arranged with the Baroness H. (in *The Daughters of the President* only the first letter of the surname is used) to give me lessons in English, to which I had no objections. But when she said she had also spoken to Fröken S., and that she was to come twice a week to give me two half-hour lessons on the piano, I snapped out at Auntie:

"I hate to play the piano! I thought I should escape that torment in Stockholm."

Whatever made me speak to Auntie as I did, I can't understand. I should have thanked her for allowing me to practice on her piano instead of saying that it was useless for me to take piano lessons as I had no talent for music, and that when I was grown, I would never touch a piano.

Auntie looked a bit surprised. "Your mother," she said, "has written and asked me to procure a music teacher for you."

Imagine! It was on the tip of my tongue to say that Mother had no business to stick her nose into my affairs, but luckily I checked myself in time. Whatever can be the matter with me! I had never even thought of my mother in that way before. It seemed as though I were somebody else and not myself.

I'm writing this in the nursery by the light of Ulla Myhrman's little lamp. It is nine o'clock in the evening. Elin and Allan are already in bed and asleep. Cousin Elin is nine years old and Allan is seven; such young children must always be in bed by seven or seven-thirty here in Stockholm. But as I am fourteen, I can sit up until half-past nine.

Auntie and Uncle have gone to a supper party, Daniel left for Upsala this morning, and Ulla has been to Uncle's room and borrowed the daily paper. She is reading it now.

Ulla is hurt, for she had counted on our playing a game of *Mariage* this evening, as we used to do when I was here before, but I said, "No."

I think it more fun to keep a diary.

In the parlour at Uncle Oriel's.

Several days have gone by, and I've had no time to write in my diary. Every day between ten and twelve I must be at the Orthopedic Institute; three hours a week I have lessons in English, and two half-hour lessons in music. Auntie is very particular to have me practice properly, and she also asks me, each time I go to Baroness, if I know my lesson.

But today I have arisen earlier than usual so that I could write. I have seated myself in the parlor, as no one comes in before breakfast. I like to sit in here because it is such a beautiful room.

I have found that it is no pleasure to keep a diary unless one writes the truth. I had plenty of time to write last evening, but something happened that I was ashamed to set down. I can't understand myself. I seem to have become so wild and unruly that I've lost all control of myself, which is something I have rarely done before.

Every evening, after my cousins have gone to bed, Auntie and I go into the parlor, she to knit at a shawl and I to crochet insertion. Auntie then tells me long stories about interesting persons she has met in Stockholm.

Sometimes Uncle comes in to smoke his long pipe while he reads the daily news. When he begins to chuckle as he reads, then Auntie and I know that Editor Lindström has said something scathing about the liberals, for to Uncle's mind liberals are the worst kind of pests.

One evening when Uncle came into the parlor he carried a small, thick book. I wondered what sort of book it could be that was so interesting as to make Uncle forget his newspaper, when he suddenly looked up at me and said:

"This book you are not to read. Remember that!"

I promised to remember, and no more was said about the matter. But yesterday morning as I sat down at the piano to run through my lesson, Uncle and Auntie came in. Uncle was so busy talking to Auntie that he paid no attention to me as I struggled with Czerny's études. He was telling Auntie

116

about a Frenchman who had attempted to murder Ludwig XIII and had been broken upon the wheel in the presence of the Court and all the servitors.

As I sat playing, I could catch only fragments of what was being said, but I had a burning desire to find out how all this had come to pass. The worst of it was, I suspected that Uncle had read it all in the book that I was forbidden to touch.

I wouldn't have touched it, either, had I been my real self. Although I have many faults, I generally keep my word.

At noon, when I return from the Institute, I have to rest for an hour. I usually lie down on the sofa in the bedroom, but yesterday that room was being cleaned; so Auntie said I could lie on the lounge in Uncle's room, as he had gone out. As I stretched myself out on the couch I saw on the table, within arm's reach, the thick little book. I picked it up and opened it to see what kind of book it was.

When I found it was only a French history, I thought it very childish of Uncle to forbid me to read it, for history is something everyone who wishes may read. I began to turn the leaves, and just as I had found the place about the torture, I heard footsteps in the hall, but I am so obtuse nowadays that it didn't occur to me that it might be Uncle. The next moment he was standing in the doorway while I lay reading the forbidden book! I never felt so embarrassed in my life.

I sprang up and quickly replaced the book on the table; then I begged Uncle's pardon for being so curious to see what sort of book it was that I should not read. Uncle, however, was not so very angry at me.

"I can understand," he said, "that you are the sort who cannot breathe unless you have your nose buried in a book. Hereafter I shall leave the key to my bookcase in the lock so that you may read Sir Walter Scott as much as you like, but you must let the other books alone."

It was very kind of Uncle, and I thanked him as graciously as I could; just the same, I feel terribly ashamed. I blush if he only looks at me. I'm afraid he must think me always disobedient, and that no one can rely on any of my promises. He does not know that I am changed and that I am no longer my real self.

In the nursery.

Soon I won't know how to behave! That about Uncle and the French history was vexatious enough, but what happened today with Auntie was even worse.

Auntie's parlor is the most attractive room I have ever seen. The floor is covered with a flowered carpet; at the windows hang frilled white curtains of embroidered tulle, and between the windows is a long mirror that extends from floor to ceiling. There is a whatnot filled with dainty porcelain figurines, an inlaid divan table, and hand-carved chairs upholstered in cloth as beautiful as a rainbow. I don't think it is the carpet or the furniture that makes the room so attractive, but the many beautiful paintings that cover the walls. There's one in particular that is most remarkable. It hangs above the parlor sofa, in the place of honor, and represents Charles Gustaf X by the deathbed of Axel Oxenstierna. The painting ought to make one feel sad, but it doesn't, as the picture is so beautifully done, with handsome people in lovely attire, and there are rich carpets and gorgeous furniture and hangings. As soon as I enter the parlor my eyes are held by that painting, and when I have gazed at it awhile, the room vanishes and I am transported into a chamber of an old castle.

Auntie is very careful of her things and protects her pretty parlor carpet with white linen runners with red borders. Only today she had laid freshly laundered floor cloths over the carpet. They were very good-looking, otherwise they would not have been allowed to lie in the same room with Axel Oxenstierna!

Auntie had just finished laying the runners and sat regarding them with approval, when I came home from the Institute. Without removing my galoshes, as I had promised to do before entering a room, I walked right across the clean linen floor cloths. Aunt Georgina glanced up quickly.

"Look behind you!" she cried. As I did so, I saw a long line of black footprints on the fresh white runners. Oh, goodness gracious, what had I done! It was the first time I had forgotten to take off my galoshes in the hall before coming into a room.

Auntie saw how distressed I was and didn't scold me much. Nor did she remove the soiled runners. I can see the tracks of my muddy galoshes whenever I pass through the parlor.

I've tried to put all thought of Marit of Sotbråten from me, for I know she is nothing but a stupid figment of my imagination, but, strange to say, when things go wrong with me, I seem to see her seated at the foot of the sofa, laughing scornfully. So I cannot help wondering if Nurse Maja has sent her here to make me stupid and boorish and bad during my stay in Stockholm.

If only I knew how to change all this! For if it lasts much longer, I fear that Uncle and Aunt will become so sick and tired of me that they will send me home. It would be a terrible disgrace to be sent home.

Monday morning
Alone in the parlour with Axel Oxenstierna.

Today I was up at seven o'clock. I had so many strange things to write about that I wanted to put them all into my diary before breakfast.

It began yesterday, shortly after two o'clock, when I stood at the window in the dining room, looking out. Although I had been in Stockholm a whole week, I marveled at the changes that had taken place since I was here five years ago. Then there was nothing to look out upon but a wilderness. It was not a real wilderness such as they have in the country, but an old garden that had fallen into decay. There was no fence around it and no gate leading into it, and no flowers or flower beds, but only a drooping tree here and there. It looked shockingly untidy! Huge piles of sand and gravel, lime and brick had been dumped there, and row upon row of ugly planks.

But now the place presents a totally different appearance. The old garden has been transformed into a large public square that is called Centralplan. On one side of the square stands the great Kirstein House, which was there five years ago. I remember it very well because the Duke of East Gothnia, a brother of Charles XV, used to pass there at this time of day. Then we always sat at the window to see the elegant royal equipage drive by.

On the other side of the square, directly opposite the Kirstein House, lies the new Central Station (the Central Station is a splendid innovation, as Elin Laurell would say). It is not only convenient to live so near the station, but it is fortunate in another way, too. If, for example, a certain student should decide to come to Stockholm some Sunday, I might catch a glimpse of him as he comes out from the railway station and crosses Centralplan.

Not that I am in love with that student, oh no! But he was so pleasant, so good-looking, and so kind that it would be a comfort to me just to see him once more.

"Selma!" my aunt called from the parlor. "Why do you stand out there alone? Come in here with us."

Two of Auntie's good friends, the Lord Chancellor's lady, Maria B. and Fröken Adele S., had come to call and had been invited to stay for coffee. I remember them very well from the last time I was here. And Fru B., a beautiful and friendly woman, said she also remembered me. Fröken S. is neither pretty nor friendly, but she has style. She didn't bother to say she remembered me. Anyhow, I like Fröken S. better, for she always says something that makes you wonder and think. Listening to her is almost as interesting as listening to Elin Laurell.

I sat in the parlor during the coffee drinking and enjoyed hearing Uncle and Fröken S. indulge in a battle of wits. All at once I happened to think of what Nurse Maja had told me, and I left the room abruptly and went back to the dining room window.

When Auntie called to me again, I was glad and returned to the parlor at once.

"Now tell us, little girl," said Fru B., "for whom you were looking when you stood a full hour at the dining room window." She laughed a little, at the same time pointing a warning finger at me. I was not used to being questioned about such things and became dreadfully embarrassed. I felt the hot blood mounting on my cheeks.

"Oh, see how she blushes!" cried Fru B., shaking her forefinger. "Now confess!"

But I couldn't tell her, or Fröken S., or Auntie or Uncle that I had been watching for an Upsala student; so I seized upon the first thing that came to my mind: "I stood there waiting to see the Duke of East Gothnia drive to Kirstein House."

"But, child," shrieked Fru B., "don't you know that there is no Duke of East Gothnia now? He became king a year ago."

I knew, of course, that Charles XV was dead and had been succeeded by his brother. It was stupid of me to say what I did, but that was the result of my embarrassment. Anyway, I don't wonder that all four of them leaned back in their chairs and burst out laughing.

"I wouldn't have believed they were so far behind the times in Värmland," Froken S. declared. "She was quite right in saying that King Oscar used to go to the Kirstein House formerly. The Academy of Music, as you know, held their meetings there, and for many years he was its president. But when he became king, he had to forego many of his former activities."

I knew that Fröken S. wanted to help me, but the others laughed just as wildly as before. So I left them and went back to the dining room window. I did not leave because I was angry. Ever since the evening I played at *priffe* with Uncle Wachenfeldt, I have not dared give way to my temper. But it seemed best to go before I uttered any more stupidities.

To think that I said I waited to see the Duke of East Gothnia when I knew so well that he was now King Oscar! It would surely end in my being sent home. Uncle and Aunt couldn't possibly put up with me any longer. So, one of these days they would take me to the railway station, buy me a ticket and put me on the train.

As these thoughts ran through my mind, I looked out at Centralplan, picturing to myself how we would appear: Auditor Afzelius walking on one side, Fru Afzelius on the other side, and I between them.

But whom should I see just then down on Centralplan but the very Upsala student who had been in the train with Daniel and me when we came to Stockholm! He stood looking up at Klara Strandgata, Number Seven, as if he knew it was there I lived.

Yes, it was surely he. I knew him at once! I tapped on the windowpane very lightly and nodded to him. He glanced up and recognized me instantly. He doffed his hat in greeting and then (it was lucky for me that the Chancellor's wife did not sit by one of the parlor windows), he threw me a kiss! When he did that, no words can describe how blissfully happy I was.

To think that anyone would throw a kiss to *me*, who am so stupid and so wicked!

That kiss made me good and kind at once. All that about Marit of Sotbråten was past and gone. I believe I had longed for that kiss the whole week. I knew now that all would be well; that hereafter I wouldn't find my music lessons such a tiresome task, nor would it occur to my aunt and uncle to send me home.

I was so happy myself that I wanted to do a kindly act for someone. So I stole quietly down the hall and through the kitchen and maids' room into the nursery. There sat old Ulla, half asleep over a newspaper, and I asked her if she would not like to play a game of *Mariage*.

"Well, I declare," she said, "if it isn't the nice little girl who lived here five years ago who has come back to us!"

THE FOURTH WEEK

Tuesday, February 11

After I cross Klara Churchyard I come to a fine large building at the corner of East Klara Kyrkogata and Odingata, which I enter. For it is there that Professor Herman Sätherberg has his Gymnasium Orthopedic Institute.

As soon as I'm inside the gate I always pause awhile. I fold my hands inside my muff and pray to God that Professor Herman Sätherberg, who is a learned and skillful physician, may soon find some way to cure me so that I won't have to go through life limping.

Then, hurrying up the stairs, I come into a large hall where there are many hangers. There I remove not only my coat and hat, but also my dress and petticoats, and put on bloomers and blouse, for otherwise, one can't exercise properly.

After that I go into the gymnasium, which is very large. There, ladders and trapezes and all kinds of gymnastic appliances hang from the walls. On the floor stand a lot of bunks with pillows, and these are the things most utilized in the forenoon by those who take remedial gymnastic treatments. But in the afternoon, I have heard, persons who are well and strong come for regular exercises; it must be then that they climb ladders and swing on trapezes.

Last autumn when I read *Neighbors* by Fredrika Bremer, I seemed to recognize the exercise she describes in that book. It would be wonderful if Fredrika Bremer had attended the same gymnasium that I do. But our exercises are not the same as those of her day. We are by no means so strenuous, nor do we have as much fun. We have no fraternities where the patients call each other by ancient Greek names, nor does it occur to us to challenge each other to fight duels.

It is a pleasure, at all events, to think of Fredrika Bremer as having been here. It is as though it boded good for another who also would write novels.

There are always many people exercising in the gymnasium. When they are all here, I think there are about a hundred going back and forth, though of course I've never counted them. All are dressed in bloomers and blouses. Some wear fine embroidered blouses, while others look as if they had jumped into a bag. There are old people and children, but the majority are nineteen or twenty years of age. Nearly all have some fault—uneven hips or a clubfoot or a stiff knee or round shoulders. Some are taking gymnastic exercises as a cure for green-sickness which they contracted by too much dancing at the Stockholm balls.

Several girls are quite nice-looking, but none so ravishingly beautiful as Louise Thyselius, who was here five years ago. *Her,* I can never forget. It would be a pleasure to have her here now to look at, for I am very much alone. I don't think there is anyone in the Institute but myself who is fourteen years old. It's like that wherever I go; I wonder where all the fourteen-year-olds have gone. At the gymnasium, they are either too old to talk to me or else so young that I wouldn't bother to talk to them.

Each one of us has a small card on which are the exercises to be taken and the name of the attendant assigned by Professor Sätherberg. There are at least ten attendants, who are easily recognized, as they dress in ordinary clothes. Each patient must have eight or nine different movements during the forenoon; so the attendants have to work until they are tired out and ready to drop.

I began with seven movements: foot-rolling, knee-bending, stretching, curtsying, et cetera. No exercise is hard, except the curtsying, for which I must stand on one leg and bend as low as I can, and that is a strain. Now that I have practiced these exercises for three weeks, I'll soon have several additional ones.

My lame leg has grown stronger already, for which I'm very thankful. Some of the patients who have been exercising all winter are now perfectly well, and they say that Professor Sätherberg is a regular wonder-worker.

Sometimes the Professor steps out of his reception room and goes the rounds of the gymnasium to see whether the attendants give us the proper movements, or to speak to some of the patients. When he comes I can't take my eyes off him.

I know that Professor Sätherberg is a poet and that he has written the lyrics to *Sing of the Student's Happiest Days* and *Happy as a Bird*, and that both poems were set to music by Prince Gustaf. But here in the gymnasium, I never hear a soul mention our Professor as the author of these splendid verses. Perhaps there is no one here but myself who knows this, but I am positive because I heard it from Uncle Oriel.

If I were not so sure that he is a poet, perhaps I could not believe it either, for Professor Sätherberg is a slight little man and not at all good-looking. His eyes are always red, and he has a sallow complexion and deep lines around the mouth. His face is sad as though he were ill. I think that a poet should be handsome and proud and radiant like Goethe. When he went skating on the River Main, he was the most distinguished-looking gentleman in all the world.

Here, in the gymnasium, at least, the Professor speaks only of crooked spines and stiff joints, but I should like to hear him talk a little about poetry. I may never have another opportunity to meet a real poet.

Several days ago, as I stood by the window looking down at Klara Churchyard, Professor Sätherberg came and stood beside me. I thought, at first, that he wished to ask me something, but he stood there looking out as though he had not seen me. As he was quite near to me and no person could hear, I made an attempt to get him to speak about something else than crooked spines. Moving a little nearer, I said as clearly as I could—for I was so nervous over my daring that I could scarcely utter the words:

"Is it a pleasure to write verse?"

Professor Sätherberg gave a start and turned to me.

"How was that?" he said. "Is there something you wish to ask me, Selma?"

I felt so timid that I would gladly have made my escape,

but somehow I managed to repeat the query: "Is it a pleasure to write verse?"

"Yes," said the Professor, and from the look he gave me, I felt that he must have thought me rather impertinent. Then in a moment he smiled. "But it is also a pleasure to straighten crooked backs and make stiff joints flexible."

Though not at all like Goethe, yet there was the look of a real poet about Professor Sätherberg when he said that. As he evidently did not wish to continue the conversation, he turned from the window and went farther back in the room.

He had given me a beautiful answer, but I did not think he was right. Now, if I could write poetry, I should never care to do anything else.

THE FIFTH WEEK

In the bedroom.

This morning I had little to do, so I sat with Auntie in her bedroom and crocheted while I listened to her stories about Stockholmers. But just as we were having the coziest time, a gentleman called. It was Squire W. of Västerås, an old friend of Uncle Oriel's who has come to Stockholm to attend a business conference.

He has brought his daughter with him, and asked if she might dine with the Afzelius family today. If Auntie would allow this, he would consider it a great favor; as he himself had to attend a business dinner, he couldn't take the girl with him. Auntie need not go to the least trouble on her account. She was a girl of just seventeen; therefore, he didn't wish her to dine alone at the hotel. It would not be proper in one so young.

Auntie laughingly assured him that Fröken W. was very welcome to have dinner with them, and added that if she felt lonely she could come whenever she wished. But the Squire thought that while Signe (that is her name) was in Stockholm she would want to visit as many shops as possible. So it was agreed that she need not come before half-past three, which is our regular dinner hour.

When this had been settled, Herr W. left. Auntie told me that it would not be an easy matter to entertain young Fröken W., for she had heard that the girl was terribly spoiled. Well, at least she would have Cook put another cake in the oven for dessert and lay a fresh cloth on the table. Auntie also advised me to change my collar and cuffs, because the W.s of Västerås are said to be very elegant and refined folk.

Just before half-past three, Uncle Oriel came home from

127

a meeting of the prison administrators, and Elin from the Alinska School (Allan attends a small primary school and was already at home). Auntie told them at once to give them time to brush up a bit before Fröken W. arrived.

"I know these small-town inhabitants," Uncle Oriel said, "and the rural folk, too. They have no sense of time. They never seem to have learned to look at a clock."

And Uncle Oriel was right—now as always. Fröken W. did not arrive on the stroke of half-past three, the time set. Nor did she come at three thirty-five; nor yet at three-forty did she appear. We wondered if she had forgotten the house number or had been run over by a brewery wagon, since she, who was from the country, naturally was not used to the heavy traffic on the streets of Stockholm.

Uncle had flung himself into the large armchair in the bedroom saying that he would take his after-dinner nap before the meal. Auntie went time and again out to the kitchen to see whether the cake had fallen or if it still held up. It was most inconsiderate of Fröken W. to be so late. But what a dreadful calamity it would be if something had befallen the girl, who is the apple of her father's eye.

At that moment there was a ring at the doorbell, and I thought how embarrassed I would be if I were a quarter of an hour late, and I felt very sorry for Fröken W.

When she came into the parlor, where we were waiting for her, she did not appear to be at all sorry. She rushed up to Auntie and Uncle; gave each a hug; kissed them on both cheeks, and asked if she might call them Aunt and Uncle. Then she kissed Elin and Allan and me right on the mouth and said we should call her Signe. She was so gay and friendly that we were all charmed with her the moment she appeared.

I need not have been the least bit anxious on her account. Fröken W. expressed no regret for being late and offered no apology. It sounded rather as though she wished to be commended for coming as early as she did. There were such wonderful shops here in Stockholm! Think of Leya's (perhaps it was best not to think of the shops!), but think of Magnusson's on Västerlånggata. Fröken W. (perhaps I ought to say Signe, since she has waived all titles between her and me) ran out into the hall and came back with all her parcels to show us what she had bought. Although Uncle Oriel had said a little while before that he was hungry enough to devour the girl herself, and Auntie had been so uneasy about the cake, they now gave themselves time to look at one purchase after another. When Fröken W. (there, I've written "Fröken W." again! Perhaps it will be best to keep on the way I have begun). When Fröken W. unrolled a dress pattern of blue linen, she gave a cry of delight. Then, directly afterward, she raised her eyebrows clear up to her hairline, and said in a voice full of anxiety that she knew the other Västerås girls would die of envy when they saw this dress pattern. She was afraid they would throw themselves into Lake Mälaren the instant they beheld it.

I did not think Fröken W. was pretty, but nevertheless, it was impossible not to keep looking at her. When Fröken W. was not talking, which was rarely, she looked like the average young girl. Mamma used to say that certain persons have a striking appearance, but that couldn't be said of Fröken W. She has light, curly hair, a sweet little mouth, white teeth, pink-and-white complexion, blue eyes as round as a ball, and a pug nose. I have seen many girls who resemble her, yet in some way she is differently constituted from the girls I have met. She was not at all embarrassed by her pug nose, but she seemed to like to show it, and to show the round baby eyes and the funny little tufts of hair that passed for eyebrows.

I gazed at Fröken W. as much as I dared without seeming to be rude, for I could learn so much from her. It was strange that she did not speak of the things one usually talks about here in Stockholm—except the shops, of course. She did not mention the royal family, the theater or the Academy of Art. She talked only of Västerås.

Uncle Oriel is over fifty years old, and aunt Georgina is at least forty, yet she talked to them as though they were but seventeen. The strange thing about it was that this seemed the proper way to approach them.

She told of a sleighing party which had afforded her much amusement, recounting for Uncle and Auntie all the stupid nonsense the gentleman had said to her while driving. Just as his love-making grew most intense, she jerked a rein so that the horse went down in the ditch and the sleigh overturned. One must have some excitement, she said, when out on a sleighing party.

When she said that, she turned her round baby eyes toward heaven, and the retroussé nose went up in the air, as much as to say she had only given him his just deserts. But her eyebrows went up in astonishment that she could have been so naughty.

Friday morning, February 21

In the sitting room.

Today I shall have to write a little more about Fröken W. I grew so sleepy yesterday while writing that I had to stop.

When there were no more parties to tell about, she took up the subject of her school and complained of her teachers— how terrible they were. They had been awfully mean to her and always had given her poor marks. She did no wrong— only walked along the street with some boys—and yet they were displeased. Jealousy, of course! She drew down her brows, her eyes grew large and dark, and her nose became almost straight. One could see so plainly how the stern old school mamselles sat at the window looking out as she passed by with her young cavaliers.

Auntie asked her whether she had ever been in Stockholm before. No, she had only been as far as Enköping. But that journey she would never forget. It had been dreadfully unpleasant because she had had such a stupid traveling companion.

You see, she was close friends with several young girls who had attended the same school at Västerås, and they had all asked her to visit them many times, but her mother and father were afraid to let her go out on the highway alone.

But last autumn she heard that the innkeeper at Enköping had brought some travelers to Västerås in his finest closed carriage; so she begged her mother to let her go with him when he returned to Enköping. Inasmuch as the carriage was a closed one, and the horses were excellent and the driver safe, she was permitted to ride those three-and-thirty miles to Enköping.

The first few miles all went well, but at Kungsåra the driver opened the door of the carriage and said that a young gentleman had reserved a place for himself and would go as far as Enköping. He was a nice and inoffensive man, the driver said, who would do her no harm.

She could not refuse the young gentleman his seat in the carriage, but certainly it was annoying for all that. Before the stranger came, she had been munching apples all the while; she was afraid that that wouldn't do now. This was her first journey, and she really didn't know what was proper or improper.

Nor did she think it would do to look at the stranger or take the slightest notice of him, so she turned toward the window and gazed down at the edge of the ditch. But the road at this point was rocky, and the carriage gave a lurch that threw her high. And then she chanced to look in the man's direction and saw that he, too, was shy. He had taken a seat directly opposite her and sat gazing out of the window.

He kept his face turned so far away that all she could see of him was a head of thin hair, plastered down, a scrawny neck, a high, loose collar, and a pale gray suit. She never could abide a pale gray suit on a gentleman.

While Fröken W. recounted how modestly the nice young man kept his eyes averted, one could fairly see how well the guileless young man conducted himself. When the road became smoother, Fröken W. sat down and again looked out of the window. But when they came to another rough place in the road, and the carriage began to shake, she was compelled against her will to cast a glance at the gray-clad man. But she had only to frown the least little bit and give him a sharp glance to make him hurry to the opposite corner and turn his back to her.

She said nothing and he said nothing, but the road was wretched, the carriage shook, and whether voluntarily or involuntarily, she did not know, but he suddenly sat down by her side and looked out through her window.

She wondered why he didn't say something. But perhaps he did not know how to begin.

Finally, as they were nearing Enköping, they could see horse-radish growing in every field along the way. It must have given him an idea, for he said in a piping voice and with a slight lisp:

"The horse-radish crop is good this year."

It was not good. On the contrary, it was very poor (according to Fröken W.), but still she said a faint, modest "Yes," for she thought it rude to contradict a strange gentleman who wished to start a polite conversation.

Again he sat looking out. She understood that he was trying hard to think of what to say next, but as nothing was seen along the way except vast fields of poor horse-radish, he could find no fresh inspiration.

"The crop of horse-radish is good this year," he piped up again—a little louder this time.

Then her patience was exhausted. What manner of man could find nothing to talk about but horse-radish?

"No, it is not good!" she shrieked and stamped her foot on the floor of the carriage.

At that, the timid young man fled to his own side of the carriage. As he did so he accidentally hit the handle of the door. It flew open, and he plunged headlong into the road.

She called to the driver to stop, but he did not hear her. He drove right on. They were just coming into Enköping, and she thought it wouldn't hurt the young man to walk that short distance. Anyhow, he had been awfully stupid!

Fröken W. glanced up at us shyly, as if to see whether we did not think she had done right. But we only laughed. She had been so indescribably amusing that we had nearly died laughing, and her facial expression was inimitable.

"My dear child, you should go on the stage," declared

Auntie.

"Do you think so, Tante? Yes—I have had my dreams of the stage, but Mamma and Papa wouldn't hear of it."

"You could become a second Fru Almlöf, but much more amusing," said Uncle Oriel. "I'll talk to your father."

"Thanks, good Uncle, but perhaps you'd better not. There is someone else, you understand, who does not wish it, either."

"Oh!" said Uncle. "In that case, I'll say no more about it."

"No," said Fröken W. with a sigh, "it would not be worth your while."

I have thought all day of Fröken W.—now I know what Aunt Georgina meant when she said that I was dull and unresponsive. I understand that she wishes me to be like Fröken W., friendly and talkative and amusing and open and natural as every young girl ought to be.

But how, how, oh how, am I to be like her!

Much as I admired Fröken W., I felt rather downhearted after she had gone because I was so unlike her. Auntie and Uncle had gone to the theater (but I have mentioned this already), invited by Squire W., and I sat in the bedchamber writing until I grew sleepy and went to bed.

I had not slept long when I awoke. Auntie had come home from the theater and stopped in the nursery to talk with Ulla, who had been sitting up for her. I heard them speak of a young girl whom they praised extravagantly. I understood, of course, they were speaking of Fröken W. That made me keep my eyes shut and pretend to be asleep. I admired Fröken W. greatly and wanted so much to be like her....

"Ulla, don't you think she is a very nice and well-brought-up young girl?" said Auntie.

"Do you know, Frua," answered Ulla, in her clear and positive voice, "I don't believe you could find a nicer or better-behaved young girl anywhere."

"No airs, nor stories about young men. She comes and goes as she should. And she is gifted, too, Ulla. Baroness H. says she speaks English remarkably well."

I was not a little astonished that the Baroness H. knew all about Fröken W. It was queer that Auntie should say she had no stories to tell about gentlemen.

"The little girl who was here today was very sweet," Auntie continued, "but, Ulla, don't you think it would be rather trying to have a person like her living in your home?"

"Yes, it would be rather trying at times," Ulla conceded.

I understood now that it was of me they were speaking, and I was so happy that I wanted to jump out of bed and give Auntie a great big hug. But then I thought that perhaps she might be angry if she knew that I had been listening—and I kept still.

THE ROYAL PALACE
STOCKHOLM

A MESSENGER FROM MÅRBACKA

The parlour at Uncle Oriel's.

Yesterday the King was crowned here in Stockholm. But it rained, so we did not see the grand event. Anyhow, I am glad there was a coronation, as it brought Aunt Lovisa to Stockholm.

I hardly think it was a pleasure for Aunt Lovisa herself. She could not see any of the coronation procession, which must have been a great disappointment to her, as she had made the long journey to Stockholm just to see royalty.

She had bought herself, in Karlstad, a pretty summer wrap and a white hat, trimmed in tulle and rosebuds. But there was no one who noticed that bit of finery, as she had to stand all the while under an umbrella.

But for me her coming was a godsend. I did not know that she was here until I got back from Upsala on Sunday. A letter from Mamma awaited me, which said that Aunt Lovisa was going to Stockholm to see the coronation and would arrive Saturday evening. Mamma also wrote that Auntie would stop with a friend of Fru Hedda Hedberg's who lives on Klarabergsgata, only a few steps from Klara Strandgata No. 7.

I was tired after the Upsala trip, and sad also, so that I was not very happy over the news that Auntie had come to Stockholm. I would have preferred to lie down on a sofa and have my sleep out, after the strain of the past two days.

But I put on my coat and hat, of course, and went out to look up my aunt. I found her one flight up in a small house. Just off the hall was a bright, prettily furnished room, and there stood Auntie before the mirror, trying on the new spring cloak and the bonnet with the rose-colored buds.

I was so surprised that I stopped at the threshold and

135

looked at her. I had never thought of Aunt Lovisa as a pretty woman, but as I saw her now she looked radiant. Not only was she beautiful, but she had brought with her something very precious. It may sound foolish to say it, but I thought that she had brought with her all Mårbacka.

She had such soft cheeks and such kindly eyes, and such small, plump hands! She couldn't have come from any place in the world but Mårbacka.

She was so good that nothing could ever make her angry, and she never worried about anything serious, but only about trifling things. She knew nothing of evil, or of the dangers and horrors that beset one on every hand in a big city like Stockholm.

She was only a Mårbacka child, a sweet old Mårbacka child.

And a Mårbacka child I was, too, though nowhere near so good as Aunt Lovisa.

It would be only a few more weeks until I could go home. That thought was a great comfort. My mind had been occupied elsewhere, and I had almost forgotten that Mårbacka existed. It was well that Aunt Lovisa had come to Stockholm, so that Mårbacka loomed large in my thoughts again.

There I would forget all that had made me sad, for at Mårbacka there were no sorrows.

ANCESTRAL TALES

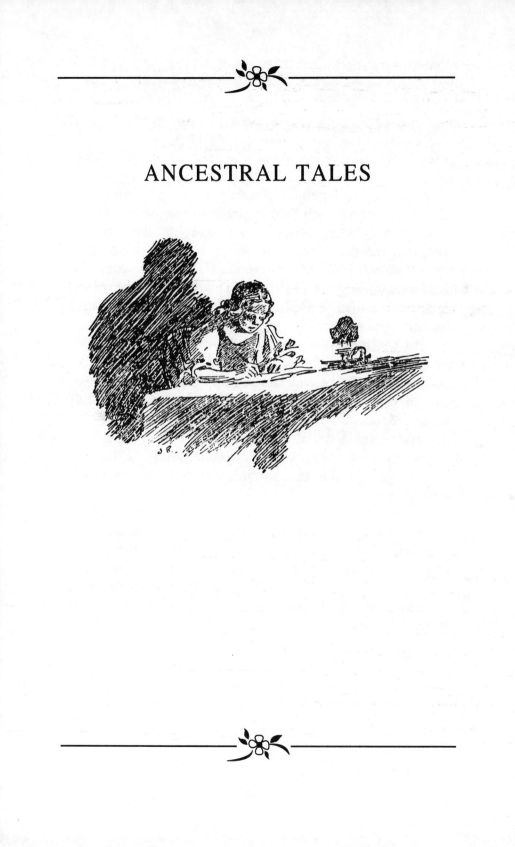

*a true story that had been passed
down...*

According to legend, Selma's paternal grandmother, Lisa Maja, was a remarkable girl in her youth as well as a captivating storyteller in her later life. The author writes of the emptiness she felt at age five, when this source of otherworldly fascination departed from the children's lives: "it seemed as if the door to a beautiful, enchanted world, where they had freely passed in and out, had been closed."

But the stories continued to be told, and characters from Mårbacka's past lives lingered on in the community's memory. There was the strong-minded woman who laid to rest a troublesome ghost with a promise that made Mårbacka a parsonage. And there was the grandmother's hard-hearted stepmother, Fru Rakvitz, whose reckoning with a prodigal gander made a lasting impression on the creator-to-be of Nils Holgersson's adventures.

In the last two stories of this section there emerges the history of another important figure in Selma's life: her father's sister, Lovisa. Aunt Lovisa's misfortune in love and consolation in Mårbacka's flower garden provided a meaningful design for the author, whose desires were similarly attached to home and family, though not in the usual way.

— G. A.

GRANDMOTHER

The year after the Strömstad[1] visit the little Mårbacka children had a great sorrow. They lost their dear grandmother.

Almost up to the very last they had sat with her on the corner sofa in the bedroom and listened to her stories and songs. They could not remember a time when their grandmother had not sung and narrated to them. It had been a glorious life. Never were children so favored.

Where their grandmother had learned her stories and ballads they did not know, but she herself believed every word of them. When she had told something very wonderful, she would look deep into the eyes of the little children and say, with utmost conviction: "All this is as true as that I see you and you see me."

One morning when the children came down to breakfast they were not allowed to go into the kitchen-bedroom as usual to say good morning to grandmother, because she was ill. All that day the corner sofa stood empty and it seemed as if the long storyless hours would never end.

A few days later the children were told their grandmother was dead, and when she lay shrouded they were brought in to kiss her hand. But they were afraid. Then someone said it was the last time they might thank Grandmother for all the pleasure she had given them. And then came the day when the stories and songs were borne away, shut up in a long black box, never to come again.

It was a sad loss to the little ones. It seemed as if the door to a beautiful, enchanted world, where they had freely passed in and out, had been closed. Now there was no one

[1]The visit to Strömstad included the memorable trip to see the Bird of Paradise. Page 17.

who knew how to open that door.

But after a while they learned to play with dolls and toys like other children, and then it may have appeared as if they no longer missed their grandmother or remembered her. But indeed she lived on in their hearts. They never tired of listening to the stories of her the old housekeeper told; they prized them as treasures they wanted to keep.

THE GHOST OF VILARSTENSBACKEN

The old housekeeper used to say, it could not have been so very long ago that Mårbacka was first laid under the plow and became a regular homestead. In the old mistress's youth, it was still within man's memory that the place had been a summer *säter* belonging to one of the old peasant farms to the west of the dale, nearer the Fryken.

But when in the world it was that the first herd of cattle grazed there and the first cattle-sheds were built, who could say? Herdsmen can hold to a place for thousands of years without leaving a trace after them. And indeed there was not much here at Mårbacka that had come down from their time.

The name Mårbacka, the old mistress believed, one of the herdsmen had given to the hilly moors below Åsberget, where they drove their horses and cattle to grass. She thought they and their animals had beaten the roads also.

That the herdsmen had broken the south road, along Åsberget, was clear, because from that direction they would have had to come with their cattle. The steep road to the east, which went straight down the mountain, was probably their work. By that they must have gone when they wished to visit *säter* folk on the other side of the mountain. The wretched road running northwest, toward Sunne, must once have been an old goat-path, and westward they could hardly have had any passage at all. To the west lay swampy bottomlands, through which ran a torturous river. When the shepherdess stood upon the flat stone outside her *säter* cabin, she could see her home-farm on the other side of the dale, but to go there, she had to go a long way round, to north or southward.

The herdsmen must have wandered up from the south mostly, for Vilarsten, or Resting-stone, where they were wont

[1]*Säter:* a crude dwelling, usually located in the mountains, for housing the animal herders.

to rest after their long tramp, still lay at the roadside, just south of the farm. But there was something about that road that made people afraid to venture out on it after dark.

At the time that Mårbacka was a summer *säter,* there lived in the parish of Sunne a priest who was so harsh and exacting that a man who had been a servant in his home a few months went and hanged himself. The priest, when he learned what had happened, without stopping to think, cut the body down and carried it out into the yard. Then, because he had touched a suicide, and for no other reason, he was regarded as polluted and disgraced. The people of Sunne would not allow him to set foot in the church, which remained closed until another clergyman was called.

The Sunne priest used also to officiate at Ämtervik, where they had a church and a little parish house but no resident clergyman. He probably thought that in an out-of-the-way place like Ämtervik no one would know of his being "unclean"; there, surely, he might celebrate the Mass, as usual. So he rode down to Ämtervik. But the evil report was there before him. As he stood at the altar intoning the Mass, murmurs ran through the congregation; the people thought him unworthy to stand in the House of God. Nor did it end there. The Ämtervik peasants felt that he had shown them great disrespect. They were as good men as the Sunne folk, they said, and would not have a priest others had repudiated.

A few among the younger peasants got together and planned to give him something to remember. But knowing it was dangerous to lay hands on a priest, they decided to wait till he set out for home. He rode alone, and there were many lonely spots along the bridle-paths between Ämtervik and Sunne where the men could lie in wait for him.

The priest must have sensed danger, for instead of taking the usual road to Sunne to the west of the dale, he took the *säter* paths eastward past Mårbacka—thinking to find his way home.

The men, ambushed at the roadside, seeing no sign of the priest, knew, of course, that he had eluded them, and thought they would have to go home without carrying out their purpose. But it happened that one of the men was a brother to the servant who had taken his own life on account of the priest, and he was not going to let him escape so easily. He seized a long stackpole which had been left standing in the field since haying time, and set off toward the marshes; the others did likewise, running and leaping across the bogs. Just below Mårbacka-säter they touched firm ground; then, hurrying southward to intercept the priest, they came upon him in the road near the Resting-stone.

It may have been their intention merely to give him a sound thrashing, but, unluckily, there was the man who had a brother to avenge. He had a sword concealed under his cloak, and when the others had pulled the priest off the horse and thrown him to the ground, the man drew his sword and cut off the priest's head.

The moment the deed was done they were filled with terror of discovery, and thought only of escape. They let the horse run loose and left the corpse lying at the roadside, to make it appear that the murder had been committed by wild robbers. Running for home by the way they had come, over the bogs, they hoped no one had seen them. They had not been on any passable road, and their venturing across the marshes would not have aroused suspicion.

Things went better than they expected. Inasmuch as the priest had been at odds with his parishioners, there was no eager search for him. When at last his body was found, the crime was attributed to outlaws. Even in death he was regarded as unclean. No one would touch the body. Since the people deemed him unfit to rest in consecrated ground, they let him lie where he was, merely covering him with sod, over which they built a cairn of large stones to prevent wild beasts digging him out.

But the priest could not find rest in the grave thus prepared for him. On moonlight nights, he would appear in the road near Resting-stone in his long cassock, holding his head between his hands. Horses saw him plainer than humans did, and would shy and rear so that riders were frequently obliged to make a long detour through the wild forest.

So long as there were only cowherds and shepherds at Mårbacka, these ghostly appearances meant very little. It was quite another matter when Mårbacka became a regular farmstead. How to lay the ghost none knew, and year after year folk had to take care not to be out on the road near the Resting-stone along about midnight.

The old mistress, however, assured the housekeeper that nowadays none need fear the headless priest. A housewife at Mårbacka, a strong-minded, determined woman, who knew a little more than the common run of folk, had laid the ghost.

That farm mistress happened to be out riding late one evening along Vilarstensbacken when, just as she expected, the ghost appeared in the road near the cairn, and made as if to bar her way.

The woman was neither awed nor frightened, and her horse was as calm and fearless as herself. She rode right up to the "spook," and began to admonish it.

"Why can't you stay where you belong!" she said. "You know well enough that no better grave awaits you. So don't imagine you will be allowed to lie in churchyard mould—you who were so corrupt when you died."

This was spoken with firm conviction, for she knew, of course, that he had been a hard man, and really considered him unworthy of decent burial.

"You have no cause to rise out of your grave and demand vengeance," she went on, "for you only got what you deserved."

When she said this, the ghost seemed to grow darker and more distinct; it looked as if ready to fall upon her. Quite undaunted, she addressed it again, determined to put an end to that nuisance.

"If you will lie still in your grave I promise you that my eldest son shall take up your calling, and become a priest. He is a good lad, and I know that he will be one of those servants of our Lord who turns people's hearts toward God and not away from Him."

She had barely uttered the first words, when the ghost

144

began to fade in the moonlight till there was nothing left of it but a faint outline, and before she had finished speaking, even that had vanished.

The Ghost of Vilarstensbacken never appeared again.

That torment luckily ended, there was increasing peace and comfort at Mårbacka. The place became as fine a farm as any in the parish, and the owners thrived and prospered.

All this, the old mistress had said, was undoubtedly true, for some years later in the beginning of the eighteenth century, a youth from Mårbacka was sent to a theological seminary, where he studied for the ministry and was finally ordained.

He called himself Morell, after his ancestral home, and in due time was made curate at Ämtervik. He settled on his family estate (Mårbacka), and was the first clergyman to reside within the parish, his predecessors all lived at Sunne and came down to Ämtervik only on specified Sundays.

The peasants of Ämtervik were glad to have their own pastor, especially one who had a home of his own so that they did not have to provide him with a living. To be sure, Mårbacka was a good distance away from the church, but that disadvantage was more than made up by the priest's being a man of independent means.

The parson's pay was small, and of that little, the lion's share went to the Dean of Sunne, so the priest would have been as poor as the proverbial mouse but for Mårbacka.

In order that this arrangement, which was for the good of both pastor and parishioners, might be perpetuated, the first clergyman at Mårbacka gave one of his daughters in marriage to a priest by the name of Lyselius, whom he made his heir to the estate and the office.

Lyselius, in his turn, did likewise: he married one of his daughters to Pastor Eric Wennervik, who later came into the property and the office.

The old mistress had said that everyone seemed to think this an excellent custom which should be kept up; even the clergymen's daughter, she thought, had been content to have it so.

145

THE GANDER

There was only one thing the children had against Pastor Wennervik—that in his late years he had married Jungfru Raklitz, the dreadful old housekeeper-person who had gone from manor to manor and been harassed and tormented by hard mistresses, until she, in her turn, became a plague and a torment.

If Pastor Wennervik must needs have married again, he should at least have thought to protect his dear daughter against the stepmother. That she was allowed to treat the girl as she saw fit, to scold and chastise her and put upon her an unreasonable amount of work—that, the children could never forgive him.

How they loved the billy goat that got drunk on dregs and butted into old Raklitz, upsetting both her and her brandy cruse. They also sided with the market folk at the Ombergshed Fair who stole her apples and shouted back to her that the Mårbacka parson was too good a man to take money from poor folk for his apples. And they gloried in the bold thief who broke into her larder after she had had a new lock put on the door, which was so big and strong it might have done for a prison gate. And they were ready to burst into tears at the thought of the poor goosey-gander!

One fine April day, in the time of Fru Raklitz, all the Mårbacka geese had been let out in the farmyard. Suddenly some wild geese came flying high above them, honking and shrieking as usual. The tame geese flapped their wings and squawked back—the way they do every spring.

As flock after flock of wild geese flew over, the tame geese grew more and more restless, and before anyone knew what was up, a big gander darted into the air and joined the wild geese in their flight.

Everyone expected that he would soon turn back, but indeed he did nothing of the sort. When he was not there by the next morning, they thought they'd never lay eyes on him again. He must have fallen prey to the fox or the eagle, they said, if he had not actually become winded and dropped dead from exhaustion. It was inconceivable that a tame goose could fly with wild geese to the far north.

Nothing was seen or heard of the gander the whole summer. But when autumn came, and the wild geese flew southward, shrieking and calling as always, the tame geese again lifted their wings and answered them.

Fru Raklitz, seeing how excited the geese were, and being more wary this time than the last, told her stepdaughter, Lisa Maja, to run out and drive the geese into the barn.

Lisa Maja had no sooner stepped into the barnyard than she heard a loud rustling noise just over her head, and almost before she had time to blink, a flock of wild geese alighted on the ground right in front of her. A big fine white gander was the leader; behind him walked a gray mother goose trailed by nine speckled goslings. The girl hardly dared move lest she frighten them away. Very cautiously, she opened the barn door and concealed herself behind it.

The goosey-gander made straight for the barn, his family following him. When they were all inside, Lisa Maja stole softly after to see where they had gone. Well, the big goosey-gander had walked right into the goose pen, and was calling and coaxing till those with him went in, too. Then he led them up to the trough, which was full of oats and water, and fell to feeding.

"See, this is what I'm used to," he seemed to be saying to his family. "This is how I have always lived...no food worries, only to step up to a full trough."

Lisa Maja quietly slipped out, shutting the door after her, and hurried back to Fru Raklitz.

"Mother dear, do come see!" she said. "The gander who flew away in the spring has come back with a wild goose and nine little goslings."

All her life she regretted having shut in the goosey-gander and told of his return. Fru Raklitz, without saying a word, hunted up the little knife which was used for killing

147

geese, and before sundown, the fine white goosey-gander, the nice gray mother goose, and all the pretty goslings were dead and plucked.

"It was a poor reward you gave our goosey-gander, Mother, for coming back to us with so many nice geese," was all she dared say.

"'Twas enough, at least, to make all the geese on this place understand what happens to those who defy me and try to run away," Fru Raklitz retorted, a malicious smile playing round her hard mouth.

THE PAYMASTER OF THE REGIMENT

F ru Raklitz's reformation may not have been so complete
after all, for the old housekeeper could never sufficiently
impress upon the little Lagerlöf children what a fortunate
thing it was for Mamselle Lisa Maja that she got so good a
husband as Paymaster Daniel Lagerlöf. He was no rich man,
but wise, and kindly, and honorable he had always been. In
him she had found just the protector she needed.

To be sure he was no priest, but his father and grandfather, his great-grandfather and great-great-grandfather
had all been clergymen and married to daughters of clergymen, so that he could claim kinship with all the old clerical
families of Värmland. Any preaching or speech-making gift
he had not inherited from his forebears, but the tendency to
guide and govern a whole community was in his blood. The
Ämtervik peasants, who at first thought ill of him because he
had married the Mårbacka parson's daughter—thereby
upsetting the old order—soon grew accustomed to having
him run the important affairs of the parish.

The children were astonished to hear the housekeeper
speak in that way of their grandfather. They had heard stories of him which were common among the people. He was
said to have been a great violinist, and in his youth, at least,
was so moody and high-strung that the humdrum of home
life wore on him and he had to go his own way.

That, the old housekeeper denied most emphatically. No,
indeed, there was nothing queer about the Paymaster of the
Regiment. She could not imagine who had put such ideas
into the children's heads. It was merely that his official
duties forced him to live away on journeys most of the time.
As Paymaster of the Regiment, once a year he had to travel
through the whole of Värmland to collect the war tax. And
not only was he Paymaster of the Regiment, but Manager of
the Kymsberg Iron Works, far up by the Norwegian bound-

ary, and all at once, he had such a good name that people were always asking him to serve as executor and administrator. Most bothersome of all had been his trusteeship for Judge Sandelin's wife, who had inherited seven foundries from Iron Master Antonsson. He had to spend months on end at these various foundries, straightening out the tangled affairs.

But as soon as ever he could get away, he hurried back to Mårbacka. If he chanced to come home some morning unobserved, he would hunt up his violin and stand outside the bedroom window and awaken his wife with music.

Now that much may have been true, perhaps, but that he ran away from home and was gone for long periods without letting anyone know his whereabouts—that was just something folks imagined, because 'twas always the wife who ruled at Mårbacka.

The children were very sorry to hear that their grandfather had been such a sober, serious, matter-of-fact person. And, of course, they had to believe what the old housekeeper told them.

Then, one evening, when their parents had gone to a party, the housemaid, who was to sit up for them, had persuaded Maja, the new nurse, who succeeded Back-Kaisa, to keep her company. They made a fire in the tile-stove of the nursery, drew up the children's little red chairs, and sat talking in whispers so as not to disturb the three little girls, who had gone to bed.

By and by the door creaked and in walked the old housekeeper. She had been wondering where the housemaid had betaken herself, and had been all through the house looking for her. She, too, drew up a chair. Anyway, she'd not be able to sleep till she knew the master and mistress were safely home.

Now that the three of them were seated by the open fire so cozy and intimate-like, the two maids seized the opportunity to ask the old housekeeper's advice in a weighty matter.

"We were just saying, Lina and I, that we ought to make dream-porridge," said Nurse Maja, "but we don't know as

150

'twould do any good."

In that way they tempted the old housekeeper to tell what had happened when Lisa Maja Wennervik made a dream-pancake.

On New Year's Eve of the last Christmas Week that Pastor Wennervik was alive, Mamselle Lisa Maja, for fun, made a dream-pancake. She had just turned seventeen, and it was time for her to be thinking of marriage. So she measured out three spoonfuls of water, three spoonfuls of meal, and three spoonfuls of salt, and stirred them together, then she poured the mixture on a hot griddle; ate as much of the pancake as she could get down, and went right to bed. She must have had some difficulty getting to sleep, though; for the salty pancake had given her an awful thirst, and to drink anything before sleeping would break the spell.

In the morning she couldn't remember whether she had dreamt anything. But later in the day, on going out on the front porch, she stopped in amazement. All at once she remembered having dreamed in the night of standing on that very spot. Two strange men—one old, one young—had come up to her. The older man had said he was Dean Lagerlöf of Arvika, and that he had come with his son to ask her if she were not thirsty and would like a drink of water. With that, the younger man had immediately stepped forward and offered her a glass of water. And she was very glad when she saw clear, fresh water, for even in her sleep her throat felt parched.

There the dream ended. But from that moment, she knew who was to be her husband; for the one who comes in the dream and offers you water when you have eaten dream-pancake, he is the one you will marry.

Mamselle Lisa Maja wondered how this could come about, for at that time she did not know anyone by the name of Lagerlöf. But one day, soon after New Year's, as she was standing at the window, a sledge came up the driveway. Suddenly she gave a cry and nipped the housekeeper by the sleeve.

"Here comes the one I saw in the dream," she said. "You'll

151

find that his name is Lagerlöf."

And 'twas just as she had said. The man in the sledge was Daniel Lagerlöf, manager of the Kymsberg Iron Works, who had come to buy hay.

The first sight of him must have been a disappointment. He was not handsome and looked so somber she did not see how she could ever like him.

He stayed the night at Mårbacka. In the morning the stableboy came in and said that a fox and two wolves had fallen into the fox-pit. None of the men on the place seemed to know what to do to get the trapped animals out, but the Kymsberg manager jumped into the pit with no weapon but a knotted stick. He dealt the wolves a couple of blows on the head, stunning them, then slipped a noose round their necks by which to draw them up.

Mamselle Lisa Maja was so taken by the courage of the man, she quite lost her heart to him. She vowed to herself, then and there, that him and none other would she have for a husband.

He, on his part, had fallen in love with her at this their first meeting, though he would not let on. He had once been engaged, it seemed, and although the betrothed was now dead, he felt that he must be true to her memory, and have no thoughts for another.

At all events, he came to Mårbacka for hay several times that winter. He soon saw that Lisa Maja had none too easy a time of it with that stepmother of hers. He felt sorry for her and wanted to help her out. But Lord o' mercy! He could not court her himself on account of the dear departed. But there was his brother Elof, who was a priest somewhere up in the Finn-forests; now he might marry her, he thought.

He brought about a meeting between his brother and Lisa Maja, which was the worst thing he could have done. The brother fell desperately in love with the girl, and could think of none but her for the rest of his life, while she loved the Kymsberg manager and had no eyes for his brother.

Pastor Lagerlöf, however, never got so far as to propose. He was commanded by his bishop to marry a person who had lived in his home several years, and to whom he had promised marriage. Fru Raklitz played a hand in that game, which ended only in misery. For when Pastor Lagerlöf could not have Lisa Maja, he took to drink, and finally became as dissolute and worthless as he had once been noble and high-minded.

Now Daniel Lagerlöf had no one to put forward as substitute. If he meant to help the Mårbacka parson's daughter, he must come to the scratch himself. Besides, he probably felt now it was better to think of the living than to mourn for the dead. So he actually plucked up courage enough to propose.

Mamselle Lisa Maja was very happy, and thought her troubles would soon be over. But before very long, her betrothed began to act strangely, as if he wished to avoid her. He seldom appeared at Mårbacka now, and when he was there he would sit silent for hours and only gaze at her, or he would take out his violin and play from the time he came until he left. At last a whole year went by without her seeing him.

If she asked him when they were to be married, he put her off with excuses. Once he said they must wait until he had earned enough to buy out the other heirs to Mårbacka. Another time he had to help put his brothers through college, and again, he thought they had better wait and see whether he'd succeed in getting the post of Paymaster of the Regiment.

He kept postponing and postponing. Now he had too much writing to do, and now too much traveling—till at last no one except Mamselle Lisa Maja herself believed they would ever be married. That made it all the harder for her. Eligible young gentlemen—from Sunne, from Ämtervik— now came a-courting. She let them all understand that they had their trouble for nothing. But some were so persistent, they came again and again, and if she forbade them the house, they would lie in wait for her at the edge of the woods, and pop out when she appeared in the road.

All the mean things they could say of Daniel Lagerlöf

they took pains to tell her. One time she heard that he consorted with the disreputable, besotten cavaliers who drove about the countryside harrying homesteads, and were the terror of all decent folk; another time she was told that he ran about in the woods like a wild animal. Some chaffed her, saying he had now got the post of Paymaster of the Regiment and could jolly well marry her, unless he'd grown tired of his bargain. Others tried to weaken her by hinting that he was after the daughter of Finn-Eric, who was reputed to be the richest man in the country.

None of that had any effect upon Lisa Maja; she was as happy and confident as ever that it would be as foretold in the dream.

Then one day a rumor reached her ears to the effect that her betrothed had said if he were only released from his engagement, he would go abroad, and learn to play the violin properly.

That impressed her as nothing else had. She went down to the stable at once to find Long-Bengt.

She said, "Now, Bengt, you must get out the chaise and drive up to Kymsberg, to fetch the Paymaster of the Regiment, for I wish to speak with him."

"Ay, be sure I'll try, Mamselle," said Long-Bengt. "But what shall I do if he won't come along willingly?"

"Tell him you dare not return without him," she said.

And Long-Bengt went.

It was a day's journey to Kymsberg, and Long-Bengt did not get back until the evening of the second day, but in the chaise with him was the Paymaster of the Regiment.

Mamselle Lisa Maja received him cordially, as usual. She asked him into the living room, and bade him sit down and rest a bit after his long journey. They would hurry with the supper, she said, as he must be hungry.

He paced up and down the room impatiently; he seemed to be waiting for the moment when he could be off.

When they were seated at table—just they two—Lisa Maja turned to him when the housekeeper came in with the food—as if she'd only been waiting for her—and asked him

154

whether it was true that he wanted to break off with her.

"Oh, yes," he answered, looking solemn as an owl. Such was his wish, of course; she should have guessed that long ago.

The blood rushed to her face. If she had not questioned him about this before, she said, it was because she firmly believed they were destined for each other. Then, with a forced laugh, he asked her what she meant by that. She flushed crimson. Now she told him in a few words about the dream-pancake, of how in a dream she had seen him and his father, and what the father had said to her.

He put down his knife and fork, and stared in amazement.

"This must be something you have just made up," he said.

"You can ask Maja Persdotter if I did not recognize you and say who you were before you were out of the sledge, the first time you came to buy hay," said Mamselle Lisa Maja, turning to the housekeeper, who was then passing round the food.

"But why haven't you spoken of this before?" he questioned her.

"That, I think, you must understand," she answered. "I did not wish to hold you by any bond but your own desire."

For a long moment he sat silent, evidently much impressed by what he had heard. Presently he asked, "Can you tell me how the man looked who said he was Dean Lagerlöf of Arvika?"

"Yes," she said, and went on to describe him. Her description of the father must have been accurate, feature for feature, for the son was so startled he involuntarily jumped up from the table.

"But my father died the year I was born," he said. "You may have heard people speak of him, perhaps?"

"I had never seen a Lagerlöf or heard of either you or your father before I met you in a dream. Ask Maja Persdotter standing there beside you if she hasn't heard me describe your father many, many times."

He went up close to her. "If only I dared believe this!" he

155

walked round the room and back to her. "Why, then *you* were the one my dear father meant for me, and not—"

What Mamselle Lisa Maja replied the old housekeeper never heard, for she saw it was time for her to be going.

The young lovers sat talking together till far into the night, and, well, that autumn they were married.

Mamselle Lisa Maja afterwards told the old housekeeper it was only his morbid conscience that had stood in the way. He had felt he would be wronging the dead sweetheart, and he had brooded over his brother Elof, and thought he had no right to happiness when the brother was so unhappy, and all on account of him.

But in her dream, he had found something to hold to, something to be guided by, which gave him the courage to do what he wished above everything.

From the day of his marriage, he was a changed man, though during the first years the old despondency came over him at times, but later he was tranquil and even-tempered as could be. A year after the wedding at Mårbacka his brother drowned, and then for a while it was pretty hard, but that, too, passed over.

The old mistress and he were married six-and-forty years, and the last thirty years of their union all was serene; there was no happier couple in the world.

The little children lay in their beds listening and delighting. Until then their grandfather had been to them no more than a wooden image, and now all at once he had come alive.

156

THE LAND OF HEART'S DESIRE

It was Lars of London, and Sven of Paris, and Magnus of Vienna, and Johan of Prague, and Per of Berlin, and Olle of Maggebysäter, the stableman and the farmboy!

Now Lars of London, Sven of Paris, Magnus of Vienna, Johan of Prague, and Per of Berlin, they were not foreigners, but farm-laborers at Mårbacka. Lieutenant Lagerlöf, in a facetious moment, had named his workmen's cottages after the principal cities of Europe.

Lars of London and Magnus of Vienna had been plowing all day in the field below the barn; Sven of Paris had fed the cows and, between times, helped on the potato land. Johan of Prague had been digging potatoes, while Per of Berlin, who had been at home all day nursing a lame back, had come over to the manor for a little diversion. The stableman had been grooming the horses, and in spare moments chopping firewood, and the farmboy had worked in the potato field. Olle of Maggebysäter was not employed at the farm; he had just come down to Mårbacka to buy a bushel of rye.

It was a drizzly day in autumn, and the men had gone into the servants' hall for the usual afternoon rest from half after four to five. Their shoes were covered with mud; their clothing was damp, and they themselves were sour and disgruntled. They had kindled a fire on the hearth, and dropped down round it. Lars of London, who had the largest croft and was the best workman, sat on the chopping-block directly in front of the fire. Magnus of Vienna, who was almost as good a worker as Lars, was sitting next to him, on one of the cobbler's stools. Sven of Paris, who thought himself quite as good as any of them, though he did tend cattle, had planted himself on the edge of the hearth, not caring whether he shut off the blaze from the others. Johan of Prague had taken the other stool, and the old man of Berlin had seated himself on a sawbuck just back of the rest. The stableman sat on the edge of the cubby-bed swinging his legs; the farmboy perched on the carpenter's bench, while Olle of Maggebysäter sat down by the door on a barrel of red ochre, resting his feet on his sack of rye.

Lars of London, Magnus of Vienna, Johan of Prague, and Sven of Paris now opened their food-bundles. They each took out a hunk of rye bread with a dab of butter on top. Drawing their sheath-knives from the belts under their leather aprons and wiping them on their trousers, they proceeded to spread their bread and cut it up, bit by bit, eating it in all comfort. The farmboy was sent over to the kitchen to fetch the fare for himself and the stableman, and came back with two halves of rye-cake, two pats of butter, and two dishes of cottage cheese. Per of Berlin, not having worked that day, had brought no lunch, and Olle of Maggebysäter had none, either; they just sat and glowered at the others.

When they had finished eating, Lars of London, Magnus of Vienna, Sven of Paris, Johan of Prague, the stableman, and the farmboy simultaneously drew from their trousers' pockets a plug of tobacco. Per of Berlin was not left out on this, for he, too, had his plug, but Olle of Maggebysäter had not even a bit of tobacco in his pocket.

The sheath-knives were again drawn. Now each man cut off a piece of his plug, laid it on his leather apron, chopped it fine, then filled his cutty-pipe.

Lars of London picked up a thin stick of wood and lighted it at the fire. After he had lit his own pipe, he gave the light to Magnus of Vienna, who passed it on to Sven of Paris; Sven of Paris handed it to Johan of Prague, who reached back and offered it to Per of Berlin: Per of Berlin leaned over so as to pass it to the stableman, who, after lighting his pipe, held the burning stick in his hand till the farmboy came across the room and took it. Olle of Maggebysäter, to be sure, had no need of a light, having neither pipe nor tobacco. The other men—now being warm and well-fed—the world began to look better to them.

But Olle Maggebysäter was three-score-and-ten, and so crippled with rheumatism that his fingers were stiff and crooked like claws; his head was drawn to one side; one leg was shorter than the other, his sight was poor; his wits were nothing to brag about, and he was toothless and ugly. Washed and combed he had certainly not been in half a year. The fringe of whiskers under his chin was full of sticks and straws. He owned a little croft up in the woods, but being nothing of a worker, he had not been able to keep poverty out of his house. Always grumpy and discontented, he had no friends. And now as the clouds of tobacco smoke rose from the other men's pipes, he muttered as if to himself:

"I've had nothin' but trouble and misery all my life, but now I've heard about a land they call America, and there I want to go."

The other men sat tranquilly musing over their pipes and made no response.

Olle of Maggebysäter continued:

"You see, 'tis like this in America—you've only to hit a rock with your stick and the rum'll come spurtin' out. That land I want to see afore I die."

The others gazed straight before them and smiled, but said nothing.

Olle of Maggebysäter talked on:

"No one can make me stick at home in this dull, miserable place, when I know there's a land where the hills are full o' rum."

The others remained persistently silent, but not a word of what Olle of Maggebysäter said was lost on them.

"The leaves of the trees in that land, they're nothin' but gold," said the poor old man. "There you don't have to do a day's work at a manor; you've only to go to the woods and pull an armful of leaves, and then you can buy yourself whatever you want. Blow me, if I don't move over there, old as I be!"

They were now in a mellow mood, all the men in the servants' hall. They saw, as it were before their eyes, that land where you tap rum from the rocks and pick gold off the trees.

The farm-bell rang. Rest-time was up. They must again go out into the wet and cold.

159

Lars of London returned to his plow; Magnus of Vienna to his; Sven of Paris, Johan of Prague, and the farmboy went back to digging potatoes; Per of Berlin betook himself home to his cottage; the stableman had to go and chop the evening's firewood, and Olle of Maggebysäter, shouldering his sack of rye, limped off to the woods.

None of them looked as glum as they did half an hour ago. There was a little glint of light in their eyes. They all felt it was good to know of a land where rum flowed from the hills and the forests were of gold, even though it lay so far away they could never reach it.

THE BRIDAL-CROWN

Mamselle Lovisa Lagerlöf used to dress the brides. Not all the girls in the parish who married came to her to be decked, only the daughters of the best peasant families. Some years there were two or three brides, and some none at all.

Formerly, when Mårbacka was a parsonage, it had been the duty of the pastor's womenfolk to deck the brides, especially those who were to be married in the church.

Mamselle Lovisa's mother and maternal grandmother and great-grandmother before her had performed this same service. It was an old custom which had been handed down.

She had inherited all the old bridal trumpery, which in the course of time, had accumulated at Mårbacka. She had a large old cupboard, in a drawer of which were treasured long strings of glass, coral, and amber beads, a collection of tortoise-shell combs that stood up eight inches from the head, and half-round pasteboard forms, covered either with stiff white satin or hand-painted flowers, in use at the period when coifs were worn. She had also a high pasteboard bridal-crown, the points of which were covered partly with gilt paper and partly with pink and green taffeta. There were wreaths of artificial roses and yards on yards of green satin ribbon sewn with flowers of pink satin. In the same drawer there were Jenny-Lind-ringlets, to be fastened on so as to fall against the face, hair pins with dangle-buttons, long ear-pendants of imitation pearls, an assortment of brass brooches, bracelets, and shoe buckles set with glass rubies, amethysts, and sapphires.

In the days when these things were in vogue, it was a responsible and laborious task to deck a bride. For days before the wedding, the bride dresser had to sit sewing flowered satin bands round the skirt and sleeves of the wedding dress. Sometimes the crown had to have fresh gilt paper, and there were paper flowers to be made, and all the brass things had to be polished till they shone like gold.

Though all the gewgaws were shoddy stuff, a peasant-bride with a high crown and a broad flower wreath on her head, with strand on strand of multi-colored beads hanging down from her neck, with flowered satin sash round her waist, with a band of gay ribbon bordering her skirt, with bangled wrists and buckled shoes, must have been the most dazzling sight one could behold.

And it was also the most becoming array for a tall, bright-eyed, rosy-cheeked peasant lass, whose figure had been developed by hard toil and whose skin was tanned by sun and wind. Thus arrayed, she carried herself with dignity and pride, as if for a space she were exalted above her kind. To the bridegroom on the wedding day she looked a queen, a veritable goddess of riches. She was the most gorgeous flower in all the meadow, and to his eyes she glittered like a jeweled casket.

When Mamselle Lovisa dressed brides, the old frippery was no longer in use. Now it had to be a natty little crown of myrtle, a thin wreath, also of myrtle, and a long white veil. Sometimes she would put a band of red satin ribbon round the waist of a plain black dress, and lend her brides her own gold brooch, gold bracelets, and watch and chain, to relieve at least a little severity of the attire.

She must, indeed, have sighed for the olden times, and felt that something was lost by being so sparing with colors and ornaments, by concealing the rugged, and sometimes rather coarse, features of the peasant brides behind a sheer, white veil. That mode suited better the pale delicate city maiden, who wished to appear before the bridegroom as something ethereal and dreamlike. She conceded that this, too, was a pretty fashion, but certainly the peasant brides would have looked much better in the old, characteristic array.

Besides, it was difficult to procure fresh myrtle for the wreath and crown. Mamselle Lovisa tried to raise a little myrtle herself, but somehow it never seemed to grow for her.

And, the brides rarely had any of their own.

Once, Mamselle Lovisa got into trouble. A middle-aged woman, one Kaisa Nilsdotter, came and asked her if she would not dress her as a bride. The woman was of the poorest peasant class, while the prospective husband was a schoolmaster. She felt that since she was making such an advantageous marriage, no less a person than Mamselle Lagerlöf should deck her. And Mamselle Lovisa was quite willing. All she asked was that the bride should help her find the myrtle.

"I am nearly out of myrtle," she said, "and do not know where to procure any."

The woman agreed to furnish the myrtle for both crown and wreath. The day before the wedding she sent a few twigs with leaves so blackened and damaged they could hardly be used for a bridal crown.

Here was a dilemma! Mamselle Lovisa stripped her own myrtles of every bit of green, but this did not go very far. The maids ran over to see what they could find on the neighboring farms, and came back with only a few poor sprigs. All the myrtle seemed to be sick that year; the leaves were black, and dropped off if one but touched them.

It would never do to bind any green but myrtle into a bridal-crown. Nice, fresh whortleberry is very like myrtle, but to wear a bridal-crown of whortleberry green would be a terrible disgrace. The bride might actually think she was not properly married.

Mamselle Lovisa laid the miserable little twigs in water to freshen them a bit, and worked far into the night on the wreath and crown. It looked a hopeless task, but she made the best of it. In the morning she quietly slipped out to the woods, but returned as she had gone—empty handed. Passing through the kitchen to her room, she averred that never had she had such difficulty trying to bind a pretty bridal-crown. The maids felt sorry for her, and offered to run to still other cottages to beg myrtle.

"No, thank you," she said, "it's too late now. The bride and groom may be here at any moment."

163

She went into her room and stuck a few more leaves into the crown and wreath where they were the barest, then showed her work to the housekeeper and the maids.

"How in the world did you do it, Mamselle Lovisa!" one exclaimed. "Why, that wreath and crown are just as pretty as those you usually make, though 'twas mostly bare sprigs and black leaves you had."

Mamselle Lovisa explained that she had freshened the leaves in water, it was only smoke and dust that had blackened them.

Shortly afterwards the bridal pair arrived. The bride was decked in Mamselle Lovisa's room. Though no longer young, the woman had a good and pleasing appearance. When she was all ready, Mamselle Lovisa conducted her into the parlor, that she might view herself in the large mirror. And she was delighted.

"I never would have thought I could look that well!" she said. Then she took out a bottle of cologne and a pretty box— gifts from the groom. The box was filled with small candies, loaf-sugar, raisins, and lozenges. These she passed round, first to Mamselle Lovisa, then to the others. All had to dab themselves with a few drops of cologne and take a piece of candy or a raisin from the box. She looked more pleased and happy than the young brides usually did, and everyone complimented her on her appearance.

In a few moments she and the bridegroom drove off to the parsonage to be married, and from there to the bride's home to celebrate.

For a time Kaisa Nilsdotter was very happy in her married life. Although her husband was much older than she, her respect for his learning was so great that she took special pride in ministering to his comfort and in making him a pleasant home. Then a rumor got afloat. It must have been started by some person at Mårbacka, but who the author was none could say. At all events, it traveled round the whole parish. At last some kind friend no doubt whispered it into the ear of Kaisa Nilsdotter.

"Mamselle Lovisa Lagerlöf bound your bridal-crown with

whortleberry green."

At first she would not believe it. Such a thing was beyond credence. But after a while she began to think back. Her bridal-crown had been as pretty as anyone else's. It had looked so fresh and green on her head. She remembered how proud she had been because a fine Mamselle had put it on her. But was the crown not much too green? The spring she was married the myrtle had all been poor, she remembered, for she had tried in vain to find some green sprays. Maybe Mamselle Lovisa had thought it was not necessary to be so very particular with one who came of such humble folk? She would never have dared offer a crown of whortleberry to the daughter of a squire.

She brooded over this and talked with her husband about it. She wondered whether they were really married, in case it was true that her crown had been of whortleberry green.

The husband tried to reason with her, but she wept and was utterly wretched, thinking herself disgraced and humiliated. Mamselle Lovisa had thought she was not fine enough to be dressed by her, so she had made her a crown of whortleberry, and now, she and all the parish were laughing at her. Her husband finally advised her to go to Mårbacka and ask Mamselle Lovisa herself about it.

She chanced to come at a most inopportune time. There was a grand party that day at Mårbacka, and when she stepped into the kitchen the maids were too busy to give her more than a short how-do-you-do. She asked for Mamselle Lovisa, who was inside with her guests, and they would not call her out. She would have to excuse them, too, for there was such a lot of company to serve. But, if she liked, she might step into Mamselle Lovisa's room, and wait there for her, which she did.

It was here the crown had been placed on her head. She remembered how happy she was that day, and now it was hard to believe there had been any deception.

Presently two maids passed through the room, each carrying a tray of filled wine glasses. They left the door ajar so that she could see into the dining room and parlor, which were full of people. It was indeed a big party, she thought. In there were, not only the gentry of Ämtervik, but the Dean's and the Doctor's folk from Sunne and Pastor Hammargren of Karlstad, the husband of Mamselle Lovisa's sister. Feeling rather embarrassed, she went to shut the door, when she caught a few words that made her stop and listen.

Lieutenant Lagerlöf, with wine glass in hand, stood in the middle of the floor announcing the betrothal of his sister Lovisa to Pastor Milén, the clergyman at Ämtervik.

Then there was much toasting and congratulating. Everyone looked happy and pleased, which was not surprising. Mamselle Lovisa was a woman of forty, and her relatives had hardly expected that she would marry. Pastor Milén was a widower with four small children who needed a mother's care. It was all so right and fitting.

Kaisa Nilsdotter had heard that when Mamselle Lovisa was young, she would not marry because she had not the heart to leave her parents. But now that they were dead, she wanted a home of her own. She had also heard that Mamselle Lovisa did not care to go far from Mårbacka, and, happily, the parsonage was but five minutes walk from there.

It sort of cut into Kaisa Nilsdotter that everything should go so well for Mamselle Lovisa—she who had made a whortleberry crown for her. Stepping back from the doorway, she saw the old housekeeper, who had come in to hear the betrothal announcement, standing just behind her. Kaisa Nilsdotter laid a heavy hand on the housekeeper's shoulder.

"I came here to find out whether Mamselle Lovisa made my bridal-crown of whortleberry green," she said. "But maybe 'twouldn't do to ask her about it on a day like this?"

The housekeeper was rather startled, but she was not one to be thrown off her guard.

"How can you say anything so idiotic, Kaisa!" she flouted. "Everyone in the house knows what a lot of bother Mamselle had with your bridal-crown. We all ran about to every cottage around here, and begged the myrtle."

Kaisa stared at her as if searching her very soul to get at the truth. "But the whole parish says so," she declared.

The old housekeeper, whose sole thought was to pacify the woman and get her out of the house, lest she disturb Mamselle Lovisa on this of all days, said:

"But I tell you, Kaisa, that as sure as Mamselle Lovisa's own bridal-crown will be of myrtle, was yours of myrtle and of nothing else."

"I'll bear those words in mind," said Kaisa. "And when I see what Mamselle Lovisa's bridal-crown is bound with, then I'll know how it was with mine."

"You can rest easy as to that," the housekeeper assured her.

The two then went into the kitchen, and Kaisa, looking quite calm now, put out her hand in farewell.

"I may as well be going," she said. "Anyhow, I don't suppose I could see Mamselle Lovisa today to speak to."

With that she was off. The housekeeper went back to her work, and, in the rush and excitement, forgot about the woman. It was not till a day or two afterward that she told Mamselle Lovisa what Kaisa Nilsdotter had said and what she herself had replied.

Mamselle Lovisa went white as a sheet.

"Oh, Maja!" she cried, "how could you say that! It would have been better to tell her that I put a few little sprays of whortleberry in her crown."

"I had to ease her mind to get her to go," the housekeeper explained.

"And so you said my crown would be of myrtle as surely as hers was. Now you'll see, Maja, there will be no bridal-crown for me!"

"Oh, you'll be married right enough, Mamselle Lovisa. Pastor Milèn is not the man to jilt you."

"Who knows? Something else might come up to prevent it."

Mamselle Lovisa worried over this a few days, and then let it pass out of mind. She had other things to think of. In six months the wedding was to take place, and she must begin at once on the household linens and the trousseau.

She set up looms, sewed, and worked monograms. She

167

finally went to Karlstad to shop, and returned with the fabric for a wedding dress and a little wire frame of a crown, to be bound with myrtle. She did not wish to use the old frame worn by so many brides, but wanted a bridal-crown of her own.

But these purchases had no sooner been made than the unexpected happened. Pastor Milén became ill and was confined to his bed a long time. When he recovered sufficiently to be up and about, he seemed strangely changed. People noticed that he did not care to talk with his betrothed, and never went the short distance to Mårbacka to see her. When summer came, he went away to a health resort. During his long absence, he never once wrote to Mamselle Lovisa. It was a time of anxiety and distress for her. She inferred from his silence that he wished to break with her, and sent him back his ring. The day this happened she said to the old housekeeper:

"Now you see, Maja, that my bridal-crown will not be bound with myrtle, either."

One day, many years later, one of the young daughters of Lieutenant Lagerlöf asked her Aunt Lovisa to lend her some of the old peasant bridal things to dress up in. Mamselle Lovisa gave her the key to the cupboard where the old treasures were kept and which had long since been removed to the storeroom upstairs.

The young girl unlocked the cupboard and pulled out a drawer. She gazed at the contents in astonishment. Before her lay not the usual gaudy trumpery, but only a parcel of tulle, some colored satin fabric, and a little wire form of a bridal crown. She saw at once that she had opened the wrong drawer; the bridal things were in the next one. Just the same, she stood a moment looking into the drawer. It wrung her heart to think that poor, unhappy Aunt Lovisa had never come to use the things lying there. She knew that for years her aunt had grieved in silence, and would not be comforted. Then something came back to memory. One day during the saddest period of her aunt's unhappiness, she had gone into her room and had found her sitting before a heap of whortle-berry green, a little wire crown in her hand. Her aunt had cut off a few sprays and was binding them round the crown, when Fru Lagerlöf came in.

"Why, Lovisa, whatever are you doing?" she had asked with a frightened look on her face.

"I was thinking," Mamselle Lovisa had said, dreamily, "that if I would be content with a crown of whortle.... but that's stupid!"

Then she had quickly jumped up, brushed aside the crown and leaves, and cried out, "I know it's all ended." Then pacing the floor and wringing her hands the while, she had moaned, "There's no help for it now."

"But, my dear Lovisa, it was only on account of his ill-ness," Fru Lagerlöf had answered.

Mamselle Lovisa had continued to pace up and down, up and down, in anguish and despair.

"If only I hadn't put whortleberry in Kaisa Nilsdotter's bridal-crown!" she had wailed.

"Come, come, Lovisa, you mustn't think that." Just then Fru Lagerlöf had caught sight of the child standing there, wide-eyed.

"Go into the other room, Selma," she had said. "Aunt Lovisa has a sorrow, and you children must not come here and disturb her."

THE GARDEN

Mamselle Lovisa certainly loved and admired her brother the Lieutenant, but she did not see why he need introduce so many changes and newfangled things. She thought Mårbacka might better be left as it was in their parents' time. What went against her most was his wanting to lay out gardens on all sides of the dwelling house.

She had been quite worried when he talked of deepening the river bed, and felt relieved when his plan miscarried. It was such a pretty sight when Ämtan overflowed and formed a lot of little shimmering lakes down in the meadows! And she wailed a good deal when her brother cleared away the field flowers. It had been a veritable feast for the eyes when one field was white with daisies, another with buttercups. And it was a great pity the cows were no longer sent to pasture in the woods. Everybody knew that such thick cream and such yellow butter as one got when they wandered in the forest were never seen when they grazed in the meadow.

In her father's time, and for hundreds of years before, it had been the custom to cut down the saplings, leave them on the ground to dry, then burn them where they lay. The following year the ashes were sown with rye, and, later, these burn-beaten clearings were covered with wild strawberries and raspberries. Mamselle Lovisa naturally took it to heart when her brother no longer burned such "falls."

"Mark my words," she said to him, "there'll soon be an end to the wild berries. Where will they grow if the woods are not burn-beaten? If all were to do as you are doing, we'd never again be able to sit of a summer's evening and watch the pretty fires round the wooded hills."

And she was not pleased with the new barn, either. Of course, she did not know very much, she said, but she had been told there was never any comfort in a stone barn.

When the new barn was finished and the old one torn

down and the Lieutenant talked of laying out a new garden, Mamselle Lovisa was beside herself.

"I trust you know what you're about," she said. "A large garden requires constant care, so you will have to figure on keeping a gardener. Unless a garden is properly tended and kept clear of weeds, one might better have none at all."

The Lieutenant let her admonitions go into one ear and out of the other. In the autumn he began tearing down the fences, which had been there since Pastor Wennervik's time—those enclosing the kitchen garden and rose garden and those surrounding the front and back yards.

"Well, this is the end of all comfort and joy in this place!" sighed Mamselle Lovisa. "Think how secure one felt when once inside all the white fences! And what fun it was for the children to run out and open the gates when company came!"

"It was less fun, though, for the one who had to keep so many fences and gates in repair," the Lieutenant replied.

He went right on with his work. When the fences were down, he plowed up the old kitchen garden and the little rose garden, the old trampled sward, the ground where the old barn had stood, and the calf ward, so as to have the grounds cleared for the laying of the garden in the spring.

"Is it true that you're going to remove the kitchen garden?" said Mamselle Lovisa. "To be sure I don't know anything, but I have heard folks say that when the apple trees are allowed to grow in the herb beds they bear well, but if one plants sod round them one can't expect much fruit."

"But dear little Lovisa, I thought you would be glad to have a real garden!"

"Glad! Should I be glad that you are destroying the old Mårbacka? Soon we won't know the place at all."

The Lieutenant thought his sister unusually contentious in this instance, which was the more surprising because she had always loved flowers and cared for all the house plants. But at that time, which was shortly after her engagement had been broken, and she was still suffering from the disappointment, he could not say a harsh word to her. All day long she paced the floor of her room, and he could hear her restless steps when he sat in the living room reading. He understood that she was not just then quite mistress of herself, and thought it a favorable sign that she took an interest in something outside her own unhappiness. It was better that she should disapprove of his garden than be continually brooding on whether she had been too hasty in sending back the betrothal ring, or whether her fiancé had turned against her because she had put a few leaves of whortleberry in Kaisa Nilsdotter's bridal-crown.

In those days there was an old landscape gardener living in Fryksdalen, who, in his prime, had been head gardener on various large estates. He had the name of being a veritable wizard at garden making, and when anyone contemplated laying out a new garden, his advice and assistance were sought.

The Lieutenant had asked him to come to Mårbacka, and in the spring, as soon as the frost was out of the ground, the old man appeared with his drawings and prints. A large corps of workmen was placed at his command; quantities of bushes and trees ordered from the Göteborg nurseries had come, and the big work was now started.

When the ground had been leveled, the gardener and the Lieutenant went about all day staking out grass plots and gravel walks. The old man informed the Lieutenant that it was no longer the custom to follow the severely regular French style. Now the paths must all be winding and the borders and flower beds in easy, graceful lines. What he had in mind for Mårbacka he called the English style, but the Lieutenant rather suspected that the style was the old man's own and not of foreign origin.

In front they laid out a big circular lawn, on one side of which they set out shrubbery in the shape of an egg, and on the other shrubbery in the form of a horn of plenty, while in the middle of the round they planted a weeping ash. Up toward the veranda, they staked out a star-shaped flower bed, placing as a guard about it four Provence-rose bushes, each on its own little round spot.

On the old sand-plot just below the kitchen windows,

they staked out a large triangle and filled it with rich soil in which they transplanted the rose bushes from the old rose garden. For of roses they could never have enough. Along the front of the house, they set out a low hedge of primroses, and two white-brier-rose bushes were given the places of honor—the one before the parlor window, the other before the front bedroom window.

The Lieutenant took such keen delight in this work that he went about with the gardener all day, and Fru Lagerlöf would snatch long moments from her sewing to go out and have a look at the garden, but Mamselle Lovisa persistently kept to her room. This delightful spring work only tended to increase her sadness. She would rather have had the old trampled sward, with its one little tangle of snowberry bushes. All these innovations seemed to her so unnecessary. But what she thought or said was immaterial; just the same, folk had managed to live at Mårbacka before. All these modern improvements only meant a lot of bother and needless expense.

But the work went on despite her disapproval. Round the stable the gardener planted a hedge of lilacs, also on three sides of the dwelling house, while along the wing he set out a hedge of spireas. That done, the Lieutenant and the gardener went at the old Wennervik kitchen garden. The fine apple trees they let stand where they were, but the ground about them was laid out in the old man's "English" style, with winding gravel paths and grass plots arranged in various designs. With much skill and calculation each grass plot was embellished with round, oblong, or triangular beds and planted with perennials. Yellow cowslips bordered blue iris; orange crown-imperials edged purpled hyssop, and encircling the red carnations was a wreath of pink bellis.

The flower beds, of course, were up round the dwelling house. Farther back, on both the north and south sides, place was made for gooseberry and currant bushes, for strawberry patches, for plum trees, pear trees, and ever so many cherry trees. At the far southern end, quite a distance away and well out of sight, lay the new kitchen garden, while at the north end was a little birch grove bordered by mountain ash and bird-cherry trees. This grove the gardener included in his design in order to create at least the suggestion of a park. He intersected the grove with many narrow winding gravel walks. In three places he cleared away the trees to make room for tables and seats. The first open space was an oblong spot with settees on all sides. Here the lady of the house was to receive her guests, and it was to be called the Tea Corner. The second was a square, with four seats round a table. That was for the master and his company, and the old man jokingly dubbed it the Toddy Corner. The third space had only a long, narrow bench. That was the Kiddies' corner.

But all this planting left Mamselle Lovisa indifferent. It may almost be said that she scorned and detested it. She had not yet set foot in the new garden.

Soon pale-green sprouts sprang up in the sod, the newly planted bushes sent forth tender, shy little leaves; the perennial plants pushed through the soil of the garden beds; oaks, chestnuts, and Lombardy poplars, which had been planted in the old barn lot, began to bud and show that they were alive.

In the midst of this busy time an unexpected difficulty arose. The old gardener was obliged to go home for a few days to see his own garden. That would not have mattered much but for the hotbed he had made in order to coax up some asters and gilly-flowers[1] for the beds in the front yard.

"Who is going to tend the hotbeds while I'm away?" said the old gardener. "You know, Lieutenant, a hotbed needs constant watching."

"I'll do it myself," the Lieutenant replied; for by that he thought himself almost a master gardener. He let the old man show him how to air and water the plants.

The morning the gardener left there was bright, strong sunshine. Along in the forenoon, the Lieutenant, in alarm, went up to the house to find his wife. As she was nowhere about, he rushed into his sister's room.

"You will have to come and help me with the hotbed,

[1]Gilly-flowers: carnations

174

Lovisa," he said. Then, remembering that Mamselle Lovisa would not even look at his garden and took no interest whatever in his work, he thought: "Oh, well, it's said now, and she can't do more than refuse."

But instead she eagerly got up and went out with him. Instantly she saw the little plants, which were wilted and drooping, she exclaimed:

"The sun is too strong on them, they must be shaded." Then she found something with which to protect them, and the plants were saved.

The next day the Lieutenant had to attend a school examination. When well on his way, he suddenly remembered the hotbed. There was the same scorching heat that day as on the previous one. Now the little plants would surely be burnt up, he thought.

The moment he got home he hurried over to the hotbed. To his surprise and delight all was well; the plants stood up, erect and sturdy. His sister had thought of the poor little things which he had neglected. He promptly decided not to forget to water and close the hotbed that evening. Sometime after supper he sprang up in alarm.

"Why, I'm forgetting the hotbed! It should have been closed this long while."

Mamselle Lovisa said nothing, but let him go see for himself. He found the glass lids down and the covers spread over them.

The following day the Lieutenant did not look at the hotbed or give it a thought. All the same, the little plants fared well. Mamselle had weeded and loosened the soil round them, watered and tended them in every way. It seemed rather strange that only she should think of the hot-bed, but for her everything sown there would have died. Of course, she wished the old gardener would return and relieve her of the work, but while he was away she had to go on with it.

He was gone longer than expected. In the meantime, the plants were growing almost too large for transplanting. There was no other course than for Mamselle Lovisa to set them out in the flower beds herself. When that much had

175

been done, what could she do but go on weeding and watering them all summer, until the gilly, petunia, aster, and snapdragon plants were in bloom!

And when the perfectly formed star before the front steps at Mårbacka appeared resplendent with bright colors, then in some mysterious way the pain was gone from Mamselle Lovisa's wounded heart. The little plants had requited the loving care she had bestowed upon them. They had given her a new interest in life, a new field of activity.

Lieutenant Lagerlöf did not have to engage a head gardener for Mårbacka; Mamselle Lovisa had inherited the old Wennervik bent, and it was she who took care of the garden. The flowers were her faithful friends; they loved her as she loved them. People wondered how she could get them to bloom and glow as in no other garden. They did not know that the flowers had caught color and sweetness from her vanished dream of happiness.

THE FATE OF MÅRBACKA

MÅRBACKA
IN 1875

THE FATE OF MÅRBACKA

MÅRBACKA
IN 1875

Perhaps these recollections, which hovered round me the last few years, were sent forth by them. I do not know, but I love to think so.

Lagerlöf wrote this on the occasion of a visit to the East Ämtervik churchyard she made on August 17, 1919, the centenary of her father's birth. There rested her Grandmother, Father, Mother, Aunt Lovisa, and the old housekeeper. *Mårbacka*, the first volume of her memoirs, was about to go to print. That fall, for the first time since childhood, she would stay through the winter in Värmland, as she would for the rest of her life. How characteristic of Selma Lagerlöf to link her inspiration to her home and kin!

"The Return to Värmland" tells a similar story of linked desire. The death of Aunt Lovisa brings Selma and her sisters back to the land where they grew up, and tugs them with an almost instinctual yearning for home. This is the meaning that the author ascribes to Lovisa's death, and it is powerful enough to bind her resolve to recover Mårbacka.

In the decades that followed, Lagerlöf dove into her role as a landowner, dealing in cattle and pigs at the same time that her literary fame attracted distinguished visitors and people pleading for help for their causes. Lagerlöf spoke out for women's suffrage and against the Nazi terror, and was active in her local community. Meanwhile, the works of memory and imagination continued to flow from her pen. The estate never profited as a farm, though Lagerlöf marketed a popular "Mårbacka oatmeal," grown and manufactured at home. Over fifty years after her death, Mårbacka is still open to an admiring public.

— G. A.

THE "EARTHQUAKE"

At twelve o'clock, when our morning lessons are over, we always run downstairs to see Mamma. She usually sits at the small table by the window, sewing. While we watch her at her work, she will ask whether we know our lessons and whether we have been diligent and well behaved, and, of course, we always answer, "Yes."

That day I had finished a little before the others, and, after washing my slate and putting my books away, without waiting for Anna or Gerda, I hurried down to Mamma's room. When I opened the door, I did not find her in her usual place at the sewing table. She was pacing up and down the room and sobbing.

She did not weep as though she had received news of a death, but as if she were beside herself with anger and despair. Pressing her hands to her head, she cried in a voice so shrill it cut into my ears:

"He must not do it! He must not do it!"

I stand stock-still in the doorway, unable to take a step. I would never have thought that Mamma could cry like that. The floor seems to open before me, and the whole house rocks to and fro.

Had Papa or Aunt Lovisa been weeping so violently it wouldn't have been very alarming. But Mamma would never weep like that unless we were threatened with ruin, for she is so wise, and the one on whom we can always depend.

Papa sits at the writing table, following Mamma with his eyes. He too looks troubled, though not in the same way as Mamma. He tries to say something to quiet her, but she does not hear him.

When Papa sees me standing at the door, he rises quickly and comes over to me. Taking my hand, he says, "We must go now and let Mamma compose herself." Then, leading me into the dining room, he drops wearily into the rocker, while

I stand close beside him.

"Why is Mamma crying?" I ask.

Papa does not answer me at once, for he sees that I am frightened. Perhaps he thinks it would be cruel to say that this is something I could not understand.

"Your Uncle Kalle came here this morning to tell us he would have to sell Gårdsjö."

This is sad news to me as well as to my parents, for I love the place and my cousins who live there. Gårdsjö has always been to me a second home. Yet I cannot understand why Mamma should take the loss so hard.

"You know that your mother is deeply attached to Gårdsjö. The foundry estate was not so extensive at the time your maternal grandfather bought it. He had made a fortune in trade at Filipstad, but as the owner of a foundry estate, he and his family had quite a different social standing."

I have nothing to say, so I keep silence.

"My father-in-law was obliged to run up to Gårdsjö twice a year," Papa continues, "and his eldest daughter usually accompanied him. That was how we met—your mother and I."

I know, of course, what Papa will say—Mamma has many happy memories that endear the place to her, but it is not like Mamma to cry so bitterly because of bright memories.

"When we were married," Papa goes on to say, "we lived at Gårdsjö for the first few years, until my father's death, when we came to live at Mårbacka."

I shake my head. I do not see what all this has to do with Mamma's weeping.

"Don't you understand that your mother thinks it deplorable that your uncle should sell Gårdsjö?"

"Yes. But why must Uncle Kalle sell?"

"He says he's losing money every year he lives there. The forge, as you know, was shut down some time ago, and the soil does not yield enough to live upon. Mamma thinks that with the sawmill, the brickyard, and the flour mill, he ought to be able to manage. But he cannot count on them, as we are in for a long period of hard times."

I close my eyes, and I seem to feel the earth tremble. One after another of the great manorial estates crumble. Now Rottneros is falling, now Skarped, now Öjervik, Stöpafors, Lövstafors, Gylleby, and Helgeby. Herrestad has already fallen, and Gårdsjö is tottering. I begin to sense what it is that Mamma fears.

I stand there with closed eyes, Papa touches my hand.

"Go into the parlor, like a good girl, and open the door to the bedroom a trifle, to see whether Mamma has quieted down."

I go, of course, but I can't help wondering why Papa does not go himself. I know that he hates to see anyone weep, but still, he should try to comfort Mamma. I had the feeling, when I stood at the bedroom door a moment ago, that Papa was actually glad of an excuse to escape. Papa is rather helpless in some things.

And now that I am alone in the parlor, I understand why Mamma is crying. I remember what Aunt Georgina said: Mamma is worried because Papa is too ill to undertake any active work. Mamma knew that bad times were coming, and had hoped and believed that Uncle Kalle would be a help and a stay to her when Papa could no longer be. But now that Uncle Kalle is leaving Gårdsjö, Mamma stands alone, with no one to go to for help.

As I open the door of the bedroom, I see Anna there. She has made Mamma lie down on the sofa and is spreading a shawl over her.

"Mamma is in good hands," I say to myself and go back to the dining room to tell Papa.

And now I see for the first time how old and broken Father is. I only wish I were rich and powerful, so that I could help him!

181

THE MESSENGER

It was just a few years after my father's death, when we had just begun to realize that we would not be in a position to keep Mårbacka. But we had not yet been able to pull ourselves together enough to think the thought through, and we had not spoken about the matter, not to each other, and not to any stranger.

One summer morning we were sitting on the veranda—all of us who were left at home—cleaning gooseberries. It was the most beautiful day one could imagine, just warm enough, no wind, and the whole sky filled with beautifully rising white clouds.

We were doubtless thinking of the same thing. Next summer it would probably not be we who would be sitting here watching the white cloud banks rise above the mountain-ash treetops. Strange eyes would feast upon the brilliancy of peonies and Provins roses. Strange hands would pick our gooseberries and gather our apples from the ground. Strange people would rejoice because they owned all this, out of which we had grown, and in which we had the roots of our whole being.

What joy would we take, hereafter, in sunshine or starry sky, in spring flowers or autumn foliage? All this was a part of Mårbacka. If we could not stay here we would lose the right appreciation of the wonders of nature. Of course, there would be green things and warmth and fine weather in other places, but that would leave us indifferent; it would not concern us.

But none of us had the courage to talk about this terrible thing which awaited us. We could still push it away and believe that it could be avoided, that we would find some way out. The situation was perhaps not so desperate. We had not yet noticed, by the attitude of our neighbors, that they knew of our worries. People came and went exactly as usual. No one seemed to think of commiserating with us.

Or if they knew, was it not queer that not one of them raised a hand to help us? To think that they would simply let us move away as if it would make no difference whatsoever! It meant nothing, then, if we left the neighborhood! And yet the family had lived here for several hundred years. But perhaps we had not been of any use. One little manor house, more or less—that was nothing to grieve over.

While we sat turning over these thoughts, each one doing his best to hide his anxiety from the others, we heard the distant notes of a clarinet.

We gave a start and listened. At first we could hardly believe our ears, that music was really being played in the quiet summer morning. "What in the world can it be?" we said. "Yes, there is certainly someone playing. It must be some itinerant musician."

But the notes reached us firm and clear. There was no mistake about it, and we did not need to be in doubt very long as to who it was who was playing. It could not be anybody but old Jan Asker, the clarinet player, who used to play the dance music at all our birthday celebrations and Christmas parties. We recognized his reels and waltzes. It was impossible to be mistaken.

Every time we had had a festival at Mårbacka, he had been a guest, as a matter of course. Nor had he ever needed to be urged. As a matter of fact, he was of a gloomy and dour disposition, but so much the greater was his need of a good party, with mirth and joy, song and dance.

But how did he happen to be out today with his clarinet? Why did he sit alone in the brilliant sunshine, playing his waltzes? We could hear from the sound that he was sitting in a little grove quite close to the house, though we could not see him.

"Probably he has been out hunting," someone said, "and now he is amusing himself by playing his old melodies while he rests."

Well, that could, of course, very well be so. We knew that he was an ardent hunter. Perhaps it did not occur to him that

183

we could hear him. Perhaps he was just playing for himself and his hunting dog.

But just as we were about to be content with this explanation, we heard him strike up the great aria from *Preciosa*: "Loneliness does not conceal me."

Oh, no, he was not playing this for himself, nor for his hunting dog!

This was for us. That aria had been one of my father's favorite pieces. Asker had had to play it for him every time he had been at our house,

After *Preciosa*, followed the seduction aria from *Don Juan*, and the "Björneborg March." They were indeed the finest numbers the old man had in his repertoire.

We sat silent and listened. We had become pale and trembling. We hardly dared look at each other. The clarinet tones were perhaps not so melodious in themselves, but they awakened so many memories.

Now the musician began to play Bellman's "Who Does Not Remember Our Brother?" And then tears came to all our eyes. To think of all the times he and other comrades had sung that song for Lieutenant Lagerlöf!

But however much we liked all this, we still found it hard to grasp the real meaning. Why had the old man walked so far? Why did he sit there playing all these pieces for us?

Then suddenly my sister said, as if she had had a revelation:

"He has found out that we cannot keep Mårbacka, and he has come here to thank us for all the times he has enjoyed himself at our house."

With that, the dreadful thing was put into words, and we felt, at first, as though we had received a blow. For we had not wanted to look the matter in the face ourselves, and we had not wanted to believe that anyone else knew about it.

But we understood at once that she was right. We understood that the old man had come for that purpose.

He had come to thank us for all the bright and beautiful things which he and others had enjoyed at our house. He wanted to tell us that it had been a fountain of joy. Its jet had spouted high into the air so that many had been attracted to it and had been comforted.

We took the whole matter as if the old man had been especially sent to tell us that there was no escape, that the misfortune had to come.

But thank God, in any case, that we had heard our doom in this way. Thanks and praise be to God that the hard truth came wrapped in happy memories, in feelings of regret and gratitude!

THE RETURN TO VÄRMLAND

Some people may perhaps recall how, in the 1870s and '80s, it proved to be impossible for all those who owned ironworks or estates in Värmland to support themselves on their properties. My sister and brother-in-law, who at that time owned my old home, Mårbacka, were obliged to do like everyone else and sell the place. They surely felt as if they were committing some great wrong, because the property had never before been sold to an outsider, but there was no other way out. Many who lived on larger and more prosperous estates had been obliged to leave them in order not to become entirely impoverished. From all parts of the province, there took place a veritable exodus of ironmasters and landed proprietors. Several of the comfortable manor houses were left standing empty, or were taken over by owners who lived in only a couple of rooms and used the upper stories as granaries. In some places there were large and expensive gardens with terraces, hedges, greenhouses, huge ornamental trees, and splendid orchards. It is better not to dwell upon the fate which they met. It cuts one to the heart.

This matter of the emigration of the old gentlefolk from Värmland is a lengthy chapter, and it is not possible to go into it at this time. Once in a while, one comes upon a little birch grove where the spruce insists upon crowding in. It is of no use to pull up the spruce saplings. They come back year after year in ever-increasing numbers, while the old birches wither away. If a few little birches should sprout up, they find no comfort. The bark cracks, and they die off as fast as they can. It was certainly something of that sort which happened in Värmland during the latter part of the nineteenth century. It was probably something that was fated to be. Perhaps the time may come when the birches will return and the spruce must make way. In any case, one must never grieve over anything like that. It is a part of nature's grand housekeeping.

At that time, however, when the great upheaval took place, one did not take it as philosophically as one can do now, long afterwards. In most places as desperate fight was fought to hold on, and after the battle was lost, one went around longing and feeling the loss for years.

I, for my part, who at the time Mårbacka was sold, was a schoolteacher at Landskrona with an annual salary of a thousand kronor, and who had not published anything but a few poems which no one had paid any attention to. I raised my hands, when I heard of the sale. I took heaven to witness that from that moment, I would have no other aim and desire than to regain the property of my forefathers. How it was to be done was quite problematic, and what joy I really would have in owning the old place I never made clear to myself. There was something inside of me which wanted it to be so; it was an inner compulsion to which I could not say no.

Many years passed, however, without its appearing as though that purpose of mine could be realized. My sister and her husband moved to Falun, and I settled there, too, in order to be near my relatives. My mother came to live with me, and also my old aunt, Lovisa Lagerlöf. The members of our former household I had thus gathered around me, although in new surroundings. This contributed, naturally, toward reconciling me to the loss of Mårbacka, but there was another reason why I no longer felt the same desire to own it. I had now entered upon the career for which I had always striven, and I felt happy and grateful.

Moreover, I had no possibility of regaining the property. My income, which was sufficient for the life I led, could in no wise suffice to buy an estate and put it into shape. It had deteriorated even during my father's last years, and most likely it had hardly been improved since.

But this did not prevent me from following the vicissitudes of the estate with the greatest interest. Through letters from my old friends in Värmland, I knew that it was incessantly being sold, bought, and sold again. One of my cousins sent me, at one time, a postal card of Mårbacka, but

I could hardly make myself recognize it. Overgrown hedges, the veranda roof gone, something dismal and unkempt about it all! Was this the place where we used to be in such good spirits—where we felt that security and comfort met us as soon as we passed the old maple tree which guarded the entrance gate?

For how much did I not have to thank this poor homestead? It looked at me with questioning and reproach. "What would you be without me? Why don't you come and take care of me now, when I need you?" it whispered to me.

But what was there to do about it? Even if I had had the very best will, I had neither the power nor the ability. There was nothing else to do but push the thought of Mårbacka aside.

I succeeded, also, for long periods, in making myself think that I had completely dismissed it from my mind. But in one way or another, it knew how to make itself remembered. I recall, for instance, a beautiful spring day down in Rome. My traveling companion and I had taken a train out to Frascati and had hired a carriage to drive up through the beautiful heights in back of the city. I had all the glory of the South around me, and was not thinking at all of my old home in Värmland, but as we penetrated farther and farther into the hills and mountains, I felt a strange uneasiness. The air had become chilly and thin; on the roadside lay a grayish white patch, which must once have been a snowdrift; over the wooded ground beside us trickled little rivulets, and suddenly I saw in front of me a few alder bushes with their black cones. I became completely bewildered. Why, I was driving along the highway south of Mårbacka! I was only a little way from home!

The next moment I was myself again, but had a feeling that all the other things which I had seen down there, the whole Campagna, all of Rome, the whole of Italy, were not worth as much to me as that little clump of alder bushes which had given me this feeling of being at home, of being once more a confident and carefree child.

But, of course, I did not return to Sweden and buy back

188

Mårbacka on that account. All that was only something which told me I should not be so sure that my longing was extinct. It lived on, sure enough, although it had to keep itself hidden away.

Another time I sat in a railroad carriage and saw a lady pick out of her traveling bag a bright astrachan. It was an unusually large and splendid apple, and quite translucent. It seemed to me as if I had not seen such a glorious fruit since I was a child. In a moment, I was home again, running around the garden on a cool September morning to look for fruit under the trees. I felt on my tongue the taste of dewy-fresh, sun-saturated astrachans, and I said to myself that I must manage things so that I could regain Mårbacka in order to be able to eat, once more, its apples.

But I became most upset of all when I heard of some Värmlander who had really returned. Thus I was told a story of a foundry which was supposed to be situated somewhere in a remote corner of Värmland. In the old days it had produced iron. Now the smelter and forge had been closed for a long time, but the place had not gone to ruin on that account. A sawmill and a pulp factory had been started, and they were profitable. The manor houses remained, well kept up; the garden was better tended than ever; fields and forests were looked after in the most careful manner.

But, of course, it was not the old ironmaster's family, the one which had founded the ironworks; built the manor house, and lived there—taking joy in their work and dispensing hospitality—which now owned the place. Nowadays it was a company estate, run by a manager. The old owners had moved away to other parts of the country. They had nothing more to do with Värmland.

A single member of the old family, however, had returned to the old neighborhood. A poor and lonely spinster, she had settled down in a village in the vicinity of the ironworks. But it was said that she never went so near it that she could even see it. She had returned to the land of her memories, but she did not wish to be disturbed by the unbearable present.

When I heard this related, I felt uneasy; I felt almost

189

ashamed. That elderly daughter of an ironmaster had a deeper affection for her home than I. She was bound to it with even stronger threads, and yet she could not possibly stand in such a heavy debt of gratitude to her home as I did to mine.

At one time, I think it was in 1906 at Christmas, I received a letter from Ironmaster Ernst Chöler, who lived at Gårdsjö in Östra Ämtervik, a neighboring estate to Mårbacka. He asked whether I really did not contemplate returning to my childhood home. The place was now owned by two farmers, splendid and painstaking men who were quite well off, but they felt that they were losing money on the property and were thereby disposed to sell it at a low price. He believed it impossible that I, who had written so many beautiful things about Värmland, should not long to return to my old home.

I thought of my old father when I read that. How often had I not heard him say that only a farmer could support himself on an estate in Värmland! To take care of his property himself, together with his wife and children, and live on its produce—that was the only way. But here it seemed that two farmers, splendid and painstaking men, had not been able to make ends meet at Mårbacka. Not for a moment was I doubtful as to the answer I must give. But before sending it off, I told the two old Mårbacka people, my mother and my aunt, about the suggestion which had been made to me.

They took the matter in a very surprising manner. They were frightened and disturbed.

"You would not go and buy back Mårbacka, would you!" they exclaimed. "You must not let Chöler tempt you into misfortune." They summoned all their persuasive powers to prevent me from buying Mårbacka. I have seldom seen them so united and so eager.

They enumerated everything possible that had been difficult and disagreeable, reminded me of cold attics and entries, of the long way to the storeroom. It was dreadful how inconvenient everything had been. The milk room in one place, the potato cellar in another. And think of the water

190

which had to be drawn from the wells and carried into the kitchen in large cowls! Think of the many servant girls and hired men! And think how we had had to argue to get the firewood chopped, and how soggy it had usually been!

I listened with the greatest surprise. My aunt had said no to desirable positions and to a couple of offers of marriage so that she could stay at home. For a while my mother had made the greatest efforts to be able to retain Mårbacka.

"You don't remember how difficult it was," said my aunt. "If you had stood on the cold stone floor of the brewery house and brewed the Christmas ale, you wouldn't want to move back."

"Don't you remember how the washwomen had to stand out in the open to rinse the clothes? When they came home in the evening their skirts were frozen so stiff that they stood up by themselves. No, my child, don't think of Mårbacka!"

They pointed out how comfortable and well off we were in Falun. Light, by only turning a button—telephone, running water, parquet floors. Had I forgotten that awful floor scouring and the scoured-floor smell?

I could have told them, even at the very start, that they disturbed themselves unnecessarily, but I had been quite surprised at meeting such a resolute resistance from that direction. But then, of course, I realized that my aunt was eighty-two and my mother seventy-nine. One could not expect them to want to move and change their residence, even had it been a question of a much pleasanter place than Mårbacka.

I wrote to Ironmaster Chöler that I could not afford to buy a country estate, and I undertook something even more decisive. I secured a house of my own in the outskirts of Falun. It was not much of a place—an old, cramped house, with a fine flower garden, splendid old trees, seclusion and peace. I felt my conscience prick me when I closed the deal, but I did not want to live any longer on a paved street, and it was, of course, absolutely impossible for me to think of Mårbacka.

However that may have been, it is difficult to say how it

191

all would have ended if my old aunt had not become sick and died at Easter, 1907. It was at once clear to me that I could not think of burying her anywhere else than in the old family plot in the Östra Ämtervik churchyard in Värmland.

She had not expressed any wish in that regard. Ever since the illness had taken a serious turn, she had lain unconscious, but of course I had understood, anyway, that she wanted to return home. While I had been sitting at her bedside in the quiet sick chamber, her silent thoughts had glided into my soul. She lay dreaming of the home of her childhood, where she loved every stone, and she felt pity for it. All that she had said about not wanting to be back there— that was only the cowardly wisdom of old age. Now she felt once more the ties which bound her to the place where she had grown up. She, who was so old, had not the strength to help it to its feet again, but she could lay herself down and die for it.

Whenever I was left alone with the dying woman, the same impression came back. "I know what I am doing." That is the way I understood her thoughts. "Something is going to happen. There is a meaning in this—in my going away."

When she lay in state, the eighty-year-old was just as beautiful as she had been in her young days. But there was, in addition, in her features, a peculiar proud joy, like that of one who has emerged with victory from a bitter struggle.

Never shall I know whether there was a trace of truth in what I thought I sensed, but certain it is that I felt I was acting in full accord with the wishes of the dead when I hastily made arrangements to have her coffin taken to Östra Ämtervik, to be interred there.

It was a peculiar spring that year. Before and during Easter, it had been warm and sunny—complete summer weather. The snow had melted away, and the lakes had been cleared of ice. But as soon as Easter had passed, a cold, windy, and rainy spell began, lasting well into May. When my sister and I left Falun, the Saturday after Easter, to attend our aunt's burial at Östra Ämtervik, we got into the bad weather. The first day we traveled by rail to Kil railway station, and on the train, of course, we suffered no discomfort from the rain and wind. But the next day we were going to drive in a carriage to Östra Ämtervik.

It turned out to be a strange journey. We were not at all in a happy frame of mind when we set out, early in the morning. We had a sad errand, the weather was the worst possible, and the road which we were to take was the narrow and hilly Karlstad road which had always been the horror of travelers. Now it was softened by the thaw, and some of the hills were slippery with ice, so that the risk of driving over it was greater than usual. There was nothing encouraging either inside or outside of us, but when we had begun the trip, when the carriage wheels skidded over the smooth ledges of the Sunngård mountains, and the road twisted back and forth in the most unexpected turns, we began to smile. We found it amusing that everything had remained exactly as it had always been. We reminded each other of the trips which, in earlier days, we had made over these same mountains. Old drivers, horses, and carriages popped up from the depths of our minds. We got into a really good humor. We had had a long period of sickness in Falun that spring, and we had not felt so light-hearted for months.

In the course of time, we arrived at Gunnarsby Inn. We had not passed that way for thirty years or more, yet we recognized plainly the inn and the entire surroundings, and what was still more remarkable, the people recognized us. They began to talk about Lieutenant Lagerlöf. They asked about our brothers Daniel and Johan, who so many times had stopped at the inn on their trips to and from Karlstad, and wondered how they had gotten along in the world.

In a word, they were glad to see us, and the oldest inhabitants came in to talk with us. The reception we got was not far from making us happy, almost proud. They had evidently not forgotten us in this place where so many people had passed during the course of the long years. We and ours had left a good impression behind us.

When we were seated in the carriage again, we felt cheered up, and we looked forward to what was ahead of us

193

with better expectation. Everything possible which had seemed obliterated from our lives sprang up again. How would things look over there in Östra Ämtervik? Would everything be the same? All those whom we had known in the old days had had time to grow old, like ourselves. Should we recognize them? Should we even have a chance to meet anyone at all?

The day was a Sunday, and it had been our intention to arrive at the Östra Ämtervik church about one o'clock, when the church service would be over, so that the interment could follow immediately afterwards. But since the road was so bad we should probably be considered delayed. We should not arrive until the church people had gone away.

I seem to remember that the rain continued to fall for a good while yet. Once in a while we caught a glimpse of Lake Fryken, but it lay gray and gloomy, and gray and gloomy was the landscape around us. We were, of course, out in the ugliest time of the year. The ground was grayish brown with withered grass. Even the little patches of winter rye were still gray and winter-murky.

But all at once the rain ceased. At the same time, the carriage was rolling down a steep hill, with an open view to the north, and we saw, as in a picture, the whole Östra Ämtervik parish along the shore of the long lake. We saw the church on its hill, the little community at its foot, the deep bay, the forest-fringed parsonage point, the long valley with its frame of softly rounded hills. Our glances sped across Lake Fryken to the west, where the church stood out white against the dark Fryksdal ridge, and caught, in a bluish haze, far to the north, the outlines of the mountains around the wide Sunne plain.

"Look, look, this is Östra Ämtervik!" we exclaimed in an irresistible excitement. "It is beautiful. It is beautiful even on a day like this. Could you believe that it was so magnificent?"

My sister leaned out of the carriage to see better, and the next moment she shouted, "Do you see the flags? Can you see that they have put up the flags?"

Sure enough, flags were actually hung at half-mast at the

rectory, the schoolmaster's house, the postmaster's and the storekeeper's, and in a couple of other places.

We became excited. Tears came to our eyes. "This is what Aunt Lovisa likes," we thought.

A few moments later, we had arrived at the home of the friends who were to lodge us. And who was it if not our old nursemaid, Maja, who stood on the steps and curtsied and bade us welcome?

As we had expected, we really were an hour or so late, but the church people had not gone away on that account. As soon as we got up the church hill, we saw that the square in front of the church was black with people.

Yes, indeed, old Miss Lovisa was surely well received when she returned to her home. The coffin was carried into the church and set down in the chancel. Two mace bearers walked at the head of the procession, and so many people followed that all the pews were filled. All those who had seen and known her were to bid her welcome again, and many others in addition. It was no season for flowers, and yet I saw many little bouquets of fuchsia, callas, and geraniums. It was the cherished window plants which had had to give up both flowers and leaves.

The rector mounted the pulpit and delivered a long funeral oration. In conclusion, he added a few words about her who had returned, and about the family to which she belonged.

We sisters nodded to each other and smiled. "Old Aunt Lovisa is surely satisfied and content with all this," we thought once more.

All this time we were in the same odd state of mind. One moment, we wept because our old friend from childhood was separated from us forever, and the next, we smiled at the sight of an old acquaintance. At the same time that we listened to the preacher, we noticed that the church had been repainted, but that the organ was just as roaring and bellowing as ever, and that it was played by the same organist as twenty years ago.

Many faces had become changed during the past years,

195

and at first glance they were not easy to recognize, but our memory cleared gradually. Wasn't that a day laborer who had worked at Mårbacka during our entire childhood, and hadn't that handsome old woman been employed there as a housemaid? Over there sat the shopkeeper of Högberg and the churchwarden from Prästbol, and that tall man we had seen on the school bench in the Östanby schoolhouse.

But there was nothing at all disrespectful to the dead in the fact that we were so affected and happy to be back in our home town and to see its people about us. We knew that this was exactly what she had wanted. It was her last will which was being fulfilled.

When the coffin had been lowered into the grave, our mission was finished and we could have returned to Falun, but we said to each other that we did not want to leave Ämtervik without having seen Mårbacka. And we stayed over until the next day in order to be able to visit our old home, which is situated about six miles from the church.

It was drizzly and chilly that day, too. There was no sunshine to gild and beautify. We were really quite anxious as to how we should find Mårbacka. There one sees nothing of the proud view over Lake Fryken, nothing of the sumptuous scenery which gives beauty to the neighborhood around the church, both summer and winter.

I don't believe we exchanged many words during the journey thither. We were no doubt recalling how we had mourned when we lost our childhood home, and we were afraid that all the pain would be reawakened.

When we passed by the Resting-stone, which lies by the edge of the road where it turns in onto the Mårbacka property, and saw that it lay there undisturbed, we drew a sigh of relief. It was as though a weight had been lifted from our hearts. We should have regarded it as a great wrong if the stone had been taken away.

We saw also that the birches which grew on one side of the road, all the way from the Resting-stone to the manor house, and which had been planted by our grandfather, were still there, and this gave us a new satisfaction.

I seem to remember that as soon as we arrived on the Mårbacka property, we lost all sense of the fact that it now belonged to strangers. We felt that we were the real owners. Our ancestors had lived here, built here, broken ground here. The property was our inheritance which could not be taken away from us. I felt as one does when one has been away on a long journey. We looked around us wonderingly and inquiringly, to see whether the home had been ill-treated during our absence.

Deep down in my heart, I should think it was quite lucky that we saw Mårbacka again on such a disagreeable spring day. Had we come there on a beautiful summer day we would have mourned because Aunt Lovisa's flowers were not beaming in their beds. We would have grieved over much more than this, but on a spring day like that, one could not expect too much. The fields must, of course, lie bare; it is a part of spring. One does not pay any attention to the fact that the gravel paths are overgrown, that the lawns are full of hummocks, that the hedges are dead. In the spring one doesn't expect anything better.

We were a little surprised that the house looked so small and that the ceilings were so low. We were provoked by a few things which ought to have been better taken care of. We could not get away from the feeling that all this was ours and that we had the right to issue orders as to how things should be arranged and managed. In one of the rooms there was still wallpaper which we two had bought with our own savings and put up with our own hands. A place like that was ours, of course.

We were not especially affected by the changes and dilapidation. Neither were we transported back to the happy days of our youth. Our strongest feeling was that the estate was our property and that it was a crime against all good order that it was in the possession of strangers.

Before I left Mårbacka it was once more offered to me by a real estate agent, but again I said no. I was not able.

But on the way back, I talked with my sister about a plan which had begun to take shape in my mind. "If someone else

197

would buy the land," I said, "and I could buy just the house and the garden—then I might possibly venture. I could move back and live there in the summertime."

As a matter of fact, that is how it was arranged to begin with.

Old Aunt Lovisa was surely satisfied as she slumbered in her grave alongside her father and mother, her sisters and brothers, with the little bouquets of the parishioners on the coffin lid. She well knew that if once I returned to Mårbacka, I should never again be able to leave it.

Childhood Memories: "The Nursemaid," "The Bird of Paradise," "The Slom Season" from *Mårbacka* (1922), translated by Velma Swanston Howard and published by Doubleday, Page & Co. in 1925. "The Vow," "The Easter Witch," "The Ball at Sunne," "The Pond," "The Well," and "Elin Laurell" from *Memories of My Childhood* (1930), translated by Velma Swanston Howard and published by Doubleday, Doran & Co. in 1934. **The Stockholm Diary:** all excerpts from *The Diary of Selma Lagerlöf* (1932), translated by Velma Swanston Howard and published by Doubleday, Doran & Co. in 1936. **Ancestral Tales:** all excerpts from *Mårbacka*. **The Fate of Mårbacka:** "The Earthquake" from *Memories of My Childhood*. "The Messenger" and "The Return to Värmland" from *Harvest* (1934), translated by Florence and Naboth Hedin, published by Doubleday, Doran & Co. in 1935. Quotation, page 178, from *Mårbacka*.